图说中国梦IV

The Chinese Dream in Pictures

Series IV

扶贫的故事

Cases of Poverty Alleviation

中国新闻社图片网络中心 主编

Compiled by China News Service Photo Network Center

新世界出版社

NEW WORLD PRESS

First Edition 2018

Compiled by China News Service Photo Network Center
Translated by Yao Wenhao
Designed by Wei Dan and Wei Fangfang

ISBN 978-7-5104-6589-5

Published by
NEW WORLD PRESS
24 Baiwanzhuang Street, Beijing 100037, China

Distributed by
NEW WORLD PRESS
24 Baiwanzhuang Street, Beijing 100037, China
Tel: 86-10-68995968
Fax: 86-10-68998705
Website: www.nwp.com.cn
E-mail: nwpcd@sina.com

Printed in the People's Republic of China

图片的温度　社会的担当

图像时代，新闻图片从来都是历史与现实的投射，映照着社会进步的历史进程。

20世纪70年代，《战火中的女孩》敲响了提前结束越战的钟声；20世纪90年代，《秃鹰和饥饿的孩子》虽饱受争议，但可以肯定的是，它引起国际舆论对苏丹饥荒和内乱的极大关注；进入21世纪，叙利亚3岁小难民随父母偷渡不幸溺亡、伏尸沙滩的照片，引发了世界对叙利亚内战和难民的巨大关切……

这些历史瞬间成为摄影和图像史上的经典，在当时激起了滚滚社会浪潮，甚至在一定程度上改变了某个社会事件的进程和方向。即使时移势易，人们再看到这些照片时，心灵依然深受震撼，百感交集。

摄影大师亨利·卡蒂埃·布列松认为，摄影作品承担着重要的社会责任，每个摄影师都应怀有尊重感，都应该意识到：一幅摄影作品无论画面多么精良、技术多么到位，如果它远离了爱，远离了对人类的理解，远离了对人类命运的认知，那么它就不是一幅成功的摄影作品。

在中国，关于扶贫，关于图片，有一幅不得不提的摄影作品——摄影家解海龙拍摄的《大眼睛》。镜头定格在一个普通山村孩子的课堂上，穿着旧棉袄的小女孩，手里握着一杆笔，清澈的大眼睛里透露出对未知世界的好奇和渴求。透过这双眼睛，人们仿佛可以听到她内心的声音——我要读书。也正是这双眼睛，让“希望工程”广为人知、备受关注。从1989年10月发起到1992年4月，“希望工程”收到捐款总计仅为1200万元；然而，“大眼睛”被确定为“希望工程”的标志后短短8个月，收到的捐款就迅速突破亿元。

“决定性瞬间”和社会责任恰巧融为一张图片，也许可以引发出惊人的社会力量。原来，摄影和图片，可以发挥的，远比我们想象的要多得多。

优秀的摄影作品不仅仅是一张图片，它是一个不能被忽视的焦点，一个时代发展的缩影，一个社会前进的故事，一个历史阶段的横切面。深入地去思考那些摄影作品从表象到内里的价值，发掘它们背后的故事和意义，从而理解社会发展的变化和本质，传递对于问题的思考和积极作为的力量，让人们意识到社会的召唤和时代的责任，这也许就是读图时代图片编辑的一种使命和担当。

本书正是用一组组图片讲述正在中国大地上开展的扶贫的故事，从某些侧面、某种程度上，展示精准扶贫的进展和成果。通过摄影和图片，既可以解读出国家层面的政策规划，也能看到地方创新驱动下的扶贫新举措；既可以看到社会团体经年累月的支援，也能感受到扶贫志愿者的付出和受助者的努力；既可以看到大山深处乡村的点滴变化，也能感受到贫困地区一个个人的成长。

这里的故事，有的出自专业摄影人之手，有的则源于普通人镜头下的记录，相较于历史经典瞬间，书中的图片或许是逊色的。但精彩在于它们的真实，镜头让那些发生在偏远地区的故事走出山乡展现在世人面前，让我们知道，这个社会很多人都在关注扶贫，以爱心、信心和耐心投入到扶贫攻坚中，共同担负着社会责任和历史使命，齐心协力地推动着社会前进的步伐。那里正在发生的日新月异的变化，如沉睡许久的新芽已破土而出，正以朝气蓬勃的力量茁壮生长，迸发出的无限希望如朝阳，温暖人心。

章新新

中国新闻社社长

2018年6月

Preface

Pictures of Social Responsibility

In an age of images, news photos are reflections of history and reality that light up the process of social progress.

In the 1970s, the *Napalm Girl* defined the Vietnam War and paved the way for its early end. In the 1990s, the famine and civil strife in Sudan caught the world's attention because of *The Vulture and the Little Girl*. Just three years ago, photographs of a three-year-old Syrian boy who was drowned fleeing Syria with his parents sparked worldwide concern for the Syrian civil war and the plight of the refugees.

These epic moments in the history of photography and videography stirred up rolling tides in the international community, and to some extent, even changed the course of certain historical events. Despite the change of time and situation, the sight of these photos can still shock the soul and stir up powerful feelings.

Henri Cartier-Bresson, a master of photography, believed that each photographer should realize and respect the fact that photographs have a lot to do with social responsibility. However good and technical a photograph looks, it will not be a successful work of photographic art if it's devoid of love and shows no recognition and understanding of our common humanity and destiny.

Big Eyes by Xie Hailong depicts a little girl wearing an old cotton-padded coat, seated with a pencil in her hand in her classroom in a village primary school. Her big clear eyes burning with curiosity about and aspiration for the unknown world make us feel as if we could hear the voice in her heart: I want knowledge! Because of these eyes, the Project Hope attracted much public attention and became widely known. From its start in October 1989 to April 1992, the public service project organized by the China Youth Development Foundation (CYDF) and the Communist Youth League (CYL) Central Committee received no more than 12 million yuan. In contrast, in just eight months after *Big Eyes* became a symbol of Project Hope, the project received a total donation of more than 100 million yuan.

The striking social effect generated by the blending of "the decisive moment" and social responsibility in a single photograph awakens us to the fact that photographic and other images can work miracles beyond our imagination.

An excellent photograph is not just a picture; it is also a nonnegligible focus, the epitome of an era of development, the story of social progress and the cross section of a historical stage. In an age of images, it is the photo editor's mission and responsibility to reflect the value of such photographs from inside and out, delve into the stories and their meanings and communicate the power of active thinking and performance so that people may understand the changes and nature of social development and hear the call of society and the responsibilities of their day and age.

This book tells in pictures stories of the ongoing poverty alleviation campaign in China and exhibits the progress and achievements of targeted poverty alleviation from certain perspectives Through photography and other images, we can learn policies and plans on the national level, find out about new poverty-relief measures engineered through local innovation and visualize how social groups dole out aid year after year. We can sense the kind of contributions made by poverty-alleviation volunteers and the hard work of those being helped. We can also discover specific changes that are taking place in villages deep in the mountains and experience the growth of individuals in poverty-stricken areas.

Of the photographic stories in this book, some come from professional photographers, others from amateurs. Compared with those capturing historic moments, they may not shine as bright. The beauty of these photographs is that they unveil to the public true stories that took place in remote rural areas and let us know that many people in this society are paying attention and devoting themselves to poverty alleviation with love, faith and patience, shouldering together social responsibility and historical mission, and promoting social progress with concerted effort. Through these pictures, we see dramatic changes taking place in underdeveloped areas. Like old plants that have budded anew, these areas or regions are developing vigorously and beaming with infinite hope that warms the heart like the morning sun.

Zhang Xinxin

President of China News Service

June 2018

目　录
CONTENTS

01 摘掉“穷帽子”
产业发展脱贫
Poverty Alleviation by Developing Industry

02 自食其力　劳动致富
转移就业脱贫
Alleviating Poverty by Migration of Impoverished Laborers

03 树挪死　人挪活
易地搬迁脱贫

Alleviating Poverty by Relocating Impoverished Population

04 阻断贫困的“遗传”
教育扶贫

Eradicating “Hereditary” Poverty Through Education

05 应对因病致贫 救助在行动

健康扶贫

Relieving Poverty Caused by Illnesses

06 绿水青山就是金山银山

生态保护扶贫

Alleviating Poverty by Protecting Eco-environment

立足贫困地区资源禀赋，以市场为导向，充分发挥农民合作组织、龙头企业等市场主体作用，建立健全产业到户到人的精准扶持机制，每个贫困县建成一批脱贫带动能力强的特色产业，每个贫困乡、村形成特色拳头产品，贫困人口劳动技能得到提升，贫困户经营性、财产性收入稳定增加。

——《“十三五”脱贫攻坚规划》

Based on the resource endowment of poverty-stricken areas, we will give full play to the market-oriented entities including farmers' cooperative organizations and leading enterprises, build a system of precision poverty alleviation from industry to household and to individual. Each impoverished county will develop special industries that will boost poverty relief capacity and each impoverished township or village will develop its own competitive products. We will help improve labor skills of impoverished populations so that they will see steady growth of their business and property income.

——National Plan for Poverty Alleviation During the 13th Five-Year Plan Period (2016-2020)

摘掉“穷帽子”

产业发展脱贫

Poverty Alleviation by Developing Industry

朝气勃发 “梦里张庄”
Thriving Zhangzhuang Village

图/文　李怀正
Photos and Text by Li Huaizheng

2017年10月，走进河南省兰考县东坝头乡张庄村，孩子们天真的笑容与这里的乡村美景和谐地融合为一体。

兰考县曾是全国有名的贫困县，张庄村位于该县北部，在20世纪六七十年代风沙肆虐兰考的时期，张庄是最大的风口。2014年，这里仍是远近闻名的贫困村，711户2963口人的张庄，在册贫困户207户754人。这一年，习近平总书记来兰考视察，兰考县委、县政府做出了“三年脱贫、七年小康”的承诺。通过实施一系列精准扶贫措施，这个承诺最终实现，2017年3月，兰考县摘掉“穷帽子”，成为河南省脱贫机制建立后首个脱贫的贫困县。

脱贫摘帽，发展产业，张庄摸索出了一条属于自己的发展之路，张庄的“红色基因”和民风特色在这个过程中得到充分发挥。

50多年前，焦裕禄在张庄实现成功防风治沙，这段历史是张庄的独特资源；张庄地处黄河大堤，村舍有着典型的豫东民居特色，“红色”乡村游大有可为。经过几年的打造，张庄的“红色”乡村旅游产业链初步形成，产业上游有占地120亩的“焦裕禄精神体验基地”，下游则是已经投入经营的农户，一院一景，有茶馆、民宿、农家乐和书馆等各种休闲场地。此外，村委转包土地，建起哈密瓜种植大棚和杂果采摘园，作为“红色”乡村旅游的配套项

Children's smile mingled with rural scenic beauty in Zhangzhuang village, Lankao County, Henan Province, in October 2017.

Lankao County was ravaged by raging sandstorms between the 1960s and 1970s and Zhangzhuang Village took the worst hits. By 2014, Zhangzhuang Village remained a well-known poor village. Of the 2,963 people from 711 households, 754 people from 207 households were registered as impoverished residents. When Xi Jinping, general secretary of the Communist Party of China (CPC) Central Committee, visited the village that year, the county Party committee and government made a commitment to "alleviate poverty within three years and achieve moderate prosperity within seven years." Through a series of targeted programs, that commitment has been honored. By March 2017, Lankao County became the first county in Henan whose "shackle of poverty" had been cast off since a provincial poverty-alleviation system was established.

Shaking off the poverty shackle through industrial development is the path Zhangzhuang Village has figured out and followed. The village made full use of its revolutionary legacy and local feature during the process.

Over 50 years ago, Jiao Yulu, head of Lankao County, led the villagers of Zhangzhuang in successfully controlling the wind and sand hazards here. This episode of village history, the village's location near the Yellow River embankment and its unique residential houses have worked together to attract tourists from across the country. After years of development, a "Red" tourism industrial chain in Zhangzhuang Village has taken shape, with an eight-hectare "Jiao Yulu Spirit Experiencing Base" and various recreational slots such as tea houses, rural inns, restaurants and bookstores run by the local villagers. Besides, the villagers' committee subcontracted land to the villagers to build Hami mel-

目，既美化环境，又增加了集体收入。

在挂着"梦里张庄"大牌子的农家大院，农家院经营者介绍，这闲置了十多年的老屋经过"包装"，让很多游客品味到了张庄的独特魅力。

on greenhouses and fruit gardens as supporting projects of "Red" tourism, which has beautified the environment and increased collective income.

At a rural inn called "Fantastic Zhangzhuang Village," the owner said that his appealing property was the renovated version of an old house that had been idle for over a decade.

01

02

01 老姐俩畅谈"梦里张庄"的新生活。
02 农家饭店的大师傅在翻地种菜。

01 Chatting joyfully at "Fantastic Zhangzhuang Village."
02 Cooks from an agritainment restaurant planting vegetables.

03

04

05

06

07

03 驻村干部利用周末时间在桐花书馆义务辅导孩子们练书法，培养他们对传统文化的兴趣。桐花书馆是由旧房改造而成，包括图书室、文艺室和活动室等，免费对村民、游客开放。

04 村文化教员在桐花书馆辅导孩子们学习。

05 孩子们在桐花书馆阅读学习。

06 孩子们在村文艺室下跳棋。

07 孩子们在自家庭院里做游戏。

03 A worker teaching the kids Chinese calligraphy to cultivate their interest in traditional culture at Tonghua Library. Converted from an old house, the library includes a reading room, a recreation room and an activity room that are open to villagers and tourists for free.

04 A village instructor tutoring school children at Tonghua Library.

05 Children reading at the library.

06 Playing Chinese checkers in the recreation room.

07 Children playing in a courtyard.

08

08 孩子们在新房子前玩游戏。
09 孩子们在宽敞洁净的街道上玩耍。这几年，张庄村硬化道路，安装上路灯，铺设了下水管网。

08 Game time.
09 Children running on a neighborhood road. In recent years, concrete roads, street lamps and a drainage system have been added to Zhangzhuang Village.

09

10 孩子们在农家小院里玩耍。
11 在“梦里张庄”农家大院门口玩耍的孩子。

10 Children playing on a farmer’s courtyard.
11 Children playing at the entrance to “Fantastic Zhangzhuang Village.”

10

11

传统陶艺焕新彩
New Glow of Traditional Pottery Art

图/文　高新生
Photos and Text by Gao Xinsheng

2017年6月17日，山西省运城市新绛县千年古城绛州龙兴镇乐义村及附近村的数十名农民陶艺师正在林堂彩陶工艺厂里为美国、日本、新加坡以及北京、广州、台湾等海内外客商赶制仿古传统陶艺工艺品。林堂彩陶工艺厂是由当地省级非物质文化遗产彩古陶烧制技艺（彩绘陶制作技艺）代表性传承人赵林堂创办的。传统民间文化艺术和非物质文化遗产在当地的脱贫致富中发挥了独特的作用。

当地政府充分发挥陶艺等传统文化扶贫帮困潜力，采取“公司+农户”“文化艺术产业园（团）+农户”等新举措，发掘全县20多类近2000种传统民间文化艺术和非物质文化遗产，为3000多位农民巧匠开辟了运用传统文化技艺脱贫的新路，带动20000多位农民增收致富。

On June 17, 2017, in Xinjiang County, Shanxi Province, dozens of pottery artists from Leyi and other neighboring villages were busy making ancient-style potteries at Lintang Art Pottery for clients from the United States, Japan, Singapore, and China's Beijing, Guangzhou and Taiwan. Lintang Art Pottery was founded by Zhao Lintang, a representative inheritor of ancient colored pottery craftsmanship, a provincial intangible cultural heritage item. The traditional folk culture and art and the intangible cultural heritage have played a unique role in local poverty alleviation.

Local governments have brought into full play the potential of pottery and other forms of traditional culture in helping alleviate poverty. Local craftsmen have benefited from this new approach featuring cooperation between businesses and farmers and development of culture and art industrial parks. These measures have resulted in the development of about 2,000 forms of local traditional folk culture and art and intangible cultural heritage in more than 20 categories. So far, more than 3,000 craftsmen have benefited from their skills in these areas and they have led over 20,000 farmers to earn more income and a better living.

01

02

01 农民工艺师在雕修陶艺宝塔工艺品。

02 省级非物质文化遗产彩古陶烧制技艺（彩绘陶制作技艺）代表性传承人赵林堂在彩绘陶艺工艺品。

01 A local artist working on a pottery pagoda.

02 Zhao Lintang, inheritor of the ancient colored pottery technique, is working on a pottery vessel.

03

04

05

03 一位农民工艺师在雕制陶艺佛像。
04 农民工艺师对陶艺佛像的局部进行细致调整。
05 农民工艺师在雕修彩绘陶艺工艺品。

03 A local artist doing a pottery Buddha.
04 Detailing the forehead of a pottery Buddha.
05 A local artist doing the finishing touches of a colored pottery artwork.

06

07

06 农民工艺师在作坊里以泥为原材料雕制陶艺工艺品。

07 工艺品雕刻完成后，需放在阴凉通风处风干。

08 大件的工艺品分块制作，分别成型后，再组合成一件作品。

06 A local artist doing clay carving in his workshop.

07 Carved pottery artworks left to dry in a cool and well-ventilated area.

08 Piecing together a large artwork.

08

瑶乡的生态旅游扶贫
Alleviating Poverty Through Ecotourism in an Ethnic Yao Village

图/文　韦吉阳（图01-02）、潘志祥（图03-07）、石农兵（图08）、肖远洋（图09）
Photos and Text by Wei Jiyang (Photos 01-02), Pan Zhixiang (Photos 03-07), Shi Nongbing (Photo 08) and Xiao Yuanpan (Photo 09)

广西龙胜各族自治县龙脊镇大寨村2003年开寨接待游客，发挥龙脊梯田景观魅力，开发了以农耕梯田和民居村寨为依托的红瑶梯田旅游。村内的自然景观及浓郁的瑶族风情，吸引中外游客纷至沓来。

除了开饭店和旅店的收入，村民每年还有一份稳定的“分红”。当地村委与旅游公司签订了共同开发协议，村民负责种植水稻和维护梯田景观，旅游公司每年将门票收入按一定比例返还给大寨村，给村民分红。通过体制创新，大寨村以“生态、旅游、扶贫”三位一体的方式，带动村民脱贫致富。

如今，越来越多的地区都把旅游当作扶贫攻坚的“突破口”，旅游扶贫正以其强大的市场优势、新兴的产业活力、强劲的造血功能、巨大的带动作用，成为扶贫攻坚的崭新生力军。

Dazhai Village, Longji Town of Longsheng Multi-Ethnic Autonomous County in Guangxi has been open to tourists since 2003. The rice terraces, houses of Yao people, the natural landscapes, and the special ethnic culture here have attracted visitors from home and abroad.

Besides business income from restaurants and inns, the villagers also earn a stable annual “dividend.” The villagers' committee has signed cooperative agreements with tourism companies. As per these agreements, villagers would plant rice and maintain the terrace scenery in return for annual pro-rata dividends from the tourism companies. Through institutional innovation, Dazhai Village is helping villagers grow rich via an ecotourism-powered poverty alleviation mechanism.

Today, more and more rural areas are using tourism as a “breaking point” of poverty alleviation. Tourism is an effective approach to poverty relief thanks to a strong market edge, incipient industrial vitality, powerful production capacity and immense driving effect.

01

02

01 2014年1月28日，瑶嫂潘艳丽在自家开的农家旅馆里布置房间。
02 村民潘艳丽在网上发布旅游信息。

01 Pan Yanli, a Yao innkeeper at work in her own farmhouse inn, January 28, 2014.
02 Pan Yanli posting tourism information online.

03

03 2015年7月21日，瑶族妇女向游客展示传统纺织技艺。

04 2015年农历六月六，大寨村喜迎年度传统节日晒衣节，村民挂出一件件鲜艳夺目的红瑶服饰。晒衣节每年都吸引众多游客前来体验当地特有的民族风情。

03 Yao women showing their traditional weaving skills to tourists, July 21, 2015.

04 The sixth day of the sixth lunar month is the traditional "Fashion Show Festival." On this day, the villagers will show off their bright-red Yao costumes. The festival is an annual ethnic cultural attraction to tourists.

04

05 村民在晒衣节上表演传统文体活动顶竹杠。
06 晒衣节上，红瑶传统婚礼的送亲队伍。

05 Villagers doing a tug of war with a bamboo pole during Fashion Show Festival.
06 A Yao wedding procession during Fashion Show Festival.

05

06

07

08

09

07 晒衣节上的长发梳妆表演。
08 2017年1月15日，村民代表展示分红现金。当年，200多户村民共领取了473万元分红。
09 金坑大寨梯田风光。

07 Women showing off their hairdo skills during Fashion Show Festival.
08 Villagers and their dividend cash, January 15, 2017. That year, 200 plus local households earned a total of 4.73 million yuan in dividend.
09 Jinkeng Rice Terraces in Dazhai Village.

深山美味组团“触网”
Mountain Delicacies Sold on the Internet

图/文　李欣
Photos and Text by Li Xin

2017年11月10日，在四川省叙永县电商公共服务中心，网贸港电商公司的员工正在各司其职为“双十一”购物狂欢节奋战。

叙永县地处川滇黔结合部，是国家扶贫开发工作重点县和国家电子商务进农村综合示范县。2016年起，叙永县引进综合型农村电子商务运营服务企业，集聚和发展起30多家小微企业和150个村级服务站（其中包括90个贫困村站点），网贸港电商公司正是其中一家企业。

叙永县逐渐形成“县、乡（镇）、村”三级农村电商服务体系，通过第三方网络平台，建立起“特产扶贫馆”，其主打的柿子醋、竹笋等乌蒙山区绿色生态农副产品受到市场的欢迎。通过借力“双十一”等大型网络促销活动，2017年，叙永县全年电商交易额接近2亿元人民币。

On November 10, 2017, at the E-Commerce Public Service Center in Xuyong County, Sichuan Province, employees of the Internet Trade Port E-Commerce Company were busy preparing for the upcoming November 11 online shopping spree.

Xuyong County, located at the junction of Sichuan, Yunnan and Guizhou provinces, is one of the key counties included in the national plan for poverty alleviation and development and one of the national model counties introducing e-commerce into villages. Since 2016, Xuyong County has attracted more than 30 small and micro online businesses and has built 150 village service centers (including 90 located in impoverished villages). The Internet Trade Port E-Commerce Company is one of them.

Gradually, Xuyong County has developed a three-tier rural e-commerce service system covering county, township and village levels. Through third-party network platforms, the county has set up specialty product poverty relief centers. Its best-sellers include persimmon vinegar, bamboo shoots and other green agricultural and sideline products in the Wumeng Mountains. Through the “November 11” and other shopping promotions, Xuyong County completed close to 200 million yuan worth of online transactions in 2017.

01 一名员工正在仔细查看商品信息。
02 员工们正通过网络平台进行交易。

01 An employee checking the details of a product.
02 Employees doing online transactions.

01

02

03

03 公司的办公区里悬挂着决战“双十一”的口号。

03 In the office area of the company, a poster boosting morale for sales during the “November 11” shopping spree is shown.

04

04 两名员工按照网络订单要求，在仓库内分拣商品。

04 Sorting out items for online orders.

05

05 两名员工登记商品并装箱。

05 Registration and packaging.

06

07

06 员工在仓库内搬运商品。
07 员工确认订单商品并搬运出库。

06 Hauling the goods inside the warehouse.
07 Preparing for shipping.

加强贫困人口职业技能培训和就业服务，保障转移就业贫困人口合法权益，开展劳务协作，推进就地就近转移就业，促进已就业贫困人口稳定就业和有序实现市民化、有劳动能力和就业意愿未就业贫困人口实现转移就业。

——《“十三五”脱贫攻坚规划》

We will strengthen vocational skills training and employment services for the impoverished people and ensure the legitimate rights and interests of those who are transferred to locations where they can find jobs. We will carry out labor cooperation and help those in need find employment in areas closest to their places of origin. For the employed poor, we will ensure that they have stable jobs and acquire urban household registration in an orderly way; for the unemployed who are able and willing to work, we will help them find jobs in other places.

——*National Plan for Poverty Alleviation During the 13th Five-Year Plan Period (2016-2020)*

自食其力　劳动致富

转移就业脱贫

Alleviating Poverty by Migration of Impoverished Laborers

锦绣计划　指尖创富
Brocade Plan: Wealth at Fingertips

图/文　杨文斌（图01–05）、黄晓海（图06–08）、刘朝富（图09–12）
Photos and Text by Yang Wenbin (Photos 01-05), Huang Xiaohai (Photos 06-08) and Liu Chaofu (Photos 09-12)

贵州省实施妇女特色手工产业锦绣计划，以市场为导向，以多彩贵州旅游商品“两赛一会”——中国（贵州）国际民族民间文化旅游产品博览会能工巧匠选拔大赛与旅游商品设计大赛——为载体，以刺绣、蜡染和民族服装服饰为重点，实现民族民间特色手工产业与妇女事业同步发展。

贵州省通过“锦绣计划”，全面提升妇女手工技能，促进妇女创业就业，增加人民群众收入；通过创建妇女手工产业创意、制造、交易基地，壮大妇女特色手工产业规模，形成“小商品、大产业”“小企业、大集群”发展模式。

计划到2020年，全省妇女特色手工企业、专业合作社达到2000家，10家领军企业年产值过亿元，力争两家企业实现上市或挂牌；全省妇女特色手工产业产值达80亿元；从事特色手工产业的妇女达到60万人，带动150万人脱贫。

Guizhou Province's Brocade Plan is a market-oriented plan to develop women's specialty handicraft industry. The plan concentrates on marketing embroideries, wax dyeing ethnic costumes and other ethnic fashion through the Guizhou International Ethnic Culture and Tourism Fair, the Master of All Trades and Crafts Competition and the Tourism Product Design Competition.

Through the Brocade Plan, Guizhou Province has comprehensively elevated women's handicraft skills, promoted employment and increased people's income. By building a base for the design, production and trading of women's handicrafts, the plan aims to expand the business scale, following a development mode of "turning small products into a big industry" and "turning small businesses into large corporations."

As per the plan, Guizhou will have, by 2020, 2,000 women's specialty handicraft enterprises and specialized cooperatives, ten leading enterprises with an annual output value of over 100 million yuan and two public or listed companies. By then, total output value of women's specialty handicraft industry in the province will reach 8 billion yuan.The 600,000 women working in this industry will help 1.5 million people out of poverty.

01

02

03

01 2017年11月7日，剑河县少数民族绣娘在第六期“锦绣计划”期间参加刺绣培训。50余名苗侗等少数民族绣娘在刺绣传承人的指导下，学习苗族锡绣、苗族红绣、侗族刺绣及旅游商品设计等手工技能。

02 绣娘们在第六期“锦绣计划”切磋刺绣技艺。

03 绣娘们参加刺绣培训。

01 On November 7, 2017, an embroiderer attending the sixth training session of Jianhe County's Brocade Plan. Over 50 female embroiderers of Miao, Dong and other ethnic minorities learning Miao and Dong embroidery, souvenirs design and other skills.

02 Learning embroidery skills from each other during the sixth Brocade Plan training session.

03 Female embroiderers learning embroidery skills.

04

05

04 剑河县一名少数民族绣娘在第六期“锦绣计划”期间学习侗族刺绣。

05 “锦绣计划”培训班上展示的刺绣鞋垫手工艺品。

06 2017年7月14日，在黔东南苗族侗族自治州丹寨县万达小镇苗族蜡染传习所，来自扬武镇宰沙村的苗族妇女杨再花在培训班上学习苗族蜡染绘画技艺。丹寨县是国家级贫困县，2014年起，丹寨县开始实施“锦绣计划”。

07 苗族妇女在丹寨县妇联“锦绣计划”蜡染技艺培训班上学习蜡画刀的使用技巧。

04 Learning Dong embroidery skills during the Brocade Plan training.

05 Embroidered insoles exhibited at a training class.

06 Yang Zaihua at a Miao wax painting training school in Wanda Town in Danzhai County, Qiandongnan Miao and Dong Autonomous Prefecture on July 14, 2017. Danzhai County is a national-level impoverished county. It began its Brocade Plan in 2014.

07 Learning how to use wax painting knives.

06

07

08

09

08 当地妇女在丹寨县妇联“锦绣计划”蜡染技艺培训班上学技艺。

09 2017年12月8日，绣娘在册亨县纳福新区布依文化广场学习刺绣。

08 Wax-dyeing painting training class.

09 Embroiderers learning embroidery at the Bouyei Cultural Square in Nafu New District, Ceheng County, December 8, 2017.

10

11

10 绣娘在册亨县冗渡镇秧弄锦绣坊纺线。
11 绣娘在册亨县中华布依锦绣坊织布。
12 绣娘在册亨县冗渡镇秧弄锦绣坊制衣。

10 Embroiderers spinning at Yangnong Brocade Workshop in Ceheng County.
11 Weaving at the China Bouyei Brocade Workshop in Ceheng County.
12 A tailor making a costume at the Yangnong Brocade Workshop in Ceheng County.

12

"扶贫车间"架起致富桥
"Poverty Alleviation Workshop"

图/文　黄有安（图01）、刘勤利（图02）、马玉（图03）、何红福（图04）、吴德军（图05）、袁荣生（图06）、杜炳勋（图07）
Photos and Text by Huang You'an (Photo 01), Liu Qinli (Photo 02), Ma Yu (Photo 03), He Hongfu (Photo 04), Wu Dejun (Photo 05), Yuan Rongsheng (Photo 06) and Du Bingxun (Photo 07).

"扶贫车间"作为地方产业扶贫的探索，通过"企业+扶贫车间+贫困户"的扶贫模式，为帮助贫困地区贫困人口稳定脱贫提供了新思路。"扶贫车间"既帮助留守人员就业，让贫困群众在家门口参与体面劳动，凭劳动脱贫致富，又支撑着当地劳动密集型产业的发展，为当地企业扩大生产规模带来机遇。看到家门口脱贫致富的机会，越来越多外出务工人员带着信息、技术、资金和项目返乡创业，承租"扶贫车间"，为村集体增加了租金等收入，实现多方共赢。目前，在安徽、河南、湖南、贵州、江西、新疆等地兴建的"扶贫车间"，在助力扶贫致富中起着不可忽视的作用。

The "Poverty Alleviation Workshop," an innovative, industry-led model of poverty relief, has provided food for thought for helping the poor in rural areas shake off poverty steadily. The Workshop not only helps the left-behind people find employment and work decently close to their homes, but also fuels the development of local labor-intensive industries and brings such industries opportunities to expand their production scale. As they see opportunities to grow rich in their home villages, more and more migrant workers choose to return home to start their own businesses with information, technology, fund and projects that they have acquired in big cities. By renting the Workshop, they have added revenue to the coffers of the villages and created win-win situations for all parties concerned. Currently, Poverty Alleviation Workshops set up in Anhui, Henan, Hunan, Guizhou, Jiangxi and Xinjiang are playing a significant role in helping people shake off poverty and lead a better life.

01

02

01 2017年8月7日，在安徽省安庆市望江县太慈镇食用菌(草菇)产业扶贫基地，菇农忙着加工晾晒草菇。太慈镇党委副书记聂娜琴介绍：“该基地集食用菌(草菇)种植、技能培训、扶贫驿站、扶贫车间、太阳能光伏发电为一体，主要采取‘公司+合作社+基地+贫困户’经营模式。”

02 2017年9月16日，安徽省亳州市利辛县程家集镇新建村村民在“扶贫车间”内学习针织服饰加工技术。当地政府与企业签订结对帮扶协议，在村里建“扶贫车间”。

01 Farmers out to air-dry mushrooms, August 7, 2017. Nie Naqin, deputy Party secretary of Taici Town, Wangjiang County, Anhui Province, said that the industrial production base provides edible fungi planting technology, solar photovoltaic power generation technology, jobs and sales training through cooperation between businesses, co-ops, production bases and impoverished people.

02 September 16, 2017. Villagers from Xinjian Village, Chengjiaji Town, Lixin County, Anhui Province, learning how to knit in a “Poverty Alleviation Workshop.” The local government and an enterprise signed a contract to establish this Workshop to help the impoverished.

03

04

05

03 2017年12月5日，河南省民权县白云寺镇柏木岗村群众在“扶贫车间”加工服装。白云寺镇利用财政扶贫资金280余万元，建设7个“扶贫车间”，帮助200户贫困户成功脱贫。

04 2017年12月28日，湖南省永州市道县万家庄街道万家庄村村民在“扶贫车间”里加工钱包。道县在农村建设“造血”式就业扶贫车间60余个，带动7600余人就业，其中建档立卡贫困户1600余人。

05 2018年1月9日，来自贵州省从江县洛贯产业园区美俄易地扶贫安置小区的移民群众在一家纺织企业的“扶贫车间”里工作。从江县引进劳动密集型企业入驻安置小区附近建立“就业扶贫车间”，让搬迁居民就近上班。

03 December 5, 2017. A villager from Baimugang Village, Baiyunsi Town, Minquan County, Henan Province, making clothes at a “Poverty Alleviation Workshop.” Baiyunsi Town has utilized over 2.8 million yuan of government poverty relief fund to build seven such workshops and helped over 200 impoverished households shake off poverty.

04 December 28, 2017. Villagers from Wanjiazhuang Village, Daoxian County, Hunan Province, are making wallets at a “Poverty Alleviation Workshop.” Daoxian County has built over 60 such workshops and provided over 7,600 jobs to the impoverished. Of the employees, 1,600 have been registered for targeted poverty relief.

05 January 9, 2018. Residents of a residential quarter in Congjiang County’s Luoguan Industrial Park in Guizhou Province working in a textill mill. Congjiang County invited labor-intensive enterprises to set up “Poverty Alleviation Workshops” near the community so that the relocated people can work close to their homes.

06

07

06 2017年11月16日，江西省南丰县工业园区内，江西佰特励电子科技有限公司员工在生产车间加工电子产品。南丰县人力资源和社会保障局在该公司创建“就业扶贫车间”，目前公司有员工200余名，接纳了16名残疾人和贫困户务工。

07 2017年12月17日，新疆铁门关二十九团农民在“扶贫车间”加工农机配件。铁门关市把“扶贫车间”建到群众家门口，让贫困群众农忙时节在家务农，农闲时节进厂务工，多渠道增加收入；同时有效缓解企业“招工难、用工贵”的困境。

06 Inside the industrial park of Nanfeng County, Jiangxi Province, November 16, 2017. Employees of Jiangxi Baiteli Electronics Technology Co., Ltd. are making electronic products in the workshop. The Nanfeng County Human Resources and Social Security Bureau set up a “Poverty Alleviation Workshop” in the company. Currently, the company has over 200 employees, including 16 who have disabilities and/or are from impoverished households.

07 December 17, 2017. Farmers from the 29th Regiment in Tiemenguan City, Xinjiang, are making farm machinery parts. Tiemenguan City has built this “Poverty Alleviation Workshop” near employees' homes so that the impoverished can do farm work during busy seasons and work in the workshops during slack seasons, thus effectively solving the local problem of lack of affordable labor.

西藏首位藏族直升机飞行员加措
Gyatso, First Tibetan Helicopter Pilot from Tibet

图/文　何蓬磊
Photos and Text by He Penglei

2017年11月，藏族小伙加措顺利考取商用飞行驾照，穿上三道金色肩章的飞行服，成为西藏首位藏族直升机飞行员。

2016年，拉萨市援藏项目雪鹰通航培养中国首批藏族飞行员，挑选拉萨市贫困家庭成员作为培训对象。从小就有一个“蓝天梦”的加措顺利通过各项考核，仅用一年多时间就完成了学习任务，开启了飞行员生涯。拉萨地处高原，加措需要克服气流不稳定、缺氧等诸多不利因素。加措希望积累更多飞行经验，参与紧急救援、医疗救护等任务。

In November 2017, Gyatso, a Tibetan young man successfully obtained his commercial pilot license. He put on his pilot uniform and became the first Tibetan pilot from Tibet.

In 2016, the Snow Eagle General Aviation Company carried out a mission in Lhasa to train China's first batch of Tibetan pilots. The candidates were from local impoverished families. Gyatso, a young man who had wanted to fly since early childhood, passed all tests in a little more than a year and fulfilled his dream of being a pilot. As Lhasa is on a plateau, Gyatso needs to overcome many adversities such as instable air current and anoxia. He hopes to gain enough flying experience and be able to participate in rescue missions.

01

02

03

01 加措和其他飞行员即将开始一天的飞行任务。
02 加措在起飞前检查飞机情况。
03 加措驾驶飞机即将起飞。

01 Gyatso and other pilots are ready for their day's work.
02 Pre-flight checking.
03 Gyatso about to take off.

04

05

06

07

08

04 一位藏族老人在乘坐完直升机后为飞行员加措献上哈达。
05 加措在飞行结束后对整机进行检查。
06 加措在家中整理飞行员着装。
07 周末，加措回到在拉萨堆龙德庆村的家，为父母做饭。
08 加措在大昭寺朝佛。

04 A Tibetan elder presents a hada to Gyatso after riding with him.
05 A thorough check after the flight.
06 Gyatso checking on his uniform at home.
07 Gyatso making dinner for his parents at home in Lhasa.
08 A time of worship at the Jokhang Monastery.

食用菌合作社让贫困户致富当老板
Growing Rich on Edible Mushrooms

图/文　苗育才
Photos and Text by Miao Yucai

“无论你是因啥致贫、也不管你何等贫困，只要肯干有志气，加入蓝天食用菌专业合作社，保你脱贫致富，甚至成为老板！”这是河南省夏邑县车站镇沈庄村党支部书记、夏邑县蓝天食用菌专业合作社负责人张艳军的承诺。

为了实施产业扶贫，帮扶更多贫困农户，张艳军组建食用菌生产基地和蓝天食用菌专业合作社，包括6个标准化园区和500个蘑菇大棚。合作社以食用菌种植为平台，推出入股分红、承包分红、轮换种植、零距离就业、技术帮扶等5种帮扶模式，贫困农户可以根据自己的实际情况，从中选择一种或多种模式，加入基地和合作社，实现脱贫致富。

凭借全国最大的双孢菇生产基地年产食用菌1200万公斤、产值超亿元的规模，张艳军累计帮助周边乡镇900多个贫困户稳定脱贫，76户年收入超过10万元。

2017年12月，张艳军当选为2017河南十大年度扶贫人物。

“You will grow rich if you work hard and join Blue Sky Edible Fungi Cooperative. You can even become a business owner!” This is the promise made by Zhang Yanjun, CEO of Blue Sky Edible Fungi Cooperative and Party secretary of Shenzhuang Village, Chezhan Town, Xiayi County, Henan Province.

To provide aid to more impoverished farmers through industrial development, Zhang Yanjun built the Edible Fungi Production Base and the Blue Sky Edible Fungi Specialized Cooperative, complete with six standard industrial parks and 500 mushroom greenhouses. With edible fungi planting as the core business, the Cooperative offers five aid models: dividend from investment, dividend from contracting, shifting cultivation, zero-distance employment and technical support. Impoverished rural households can choose one or multiple models based on their own conditions to join the base and cooperative to grow rich.

With the production base that produces annually more than 12 million kilograms of edible fungi and an output value of over 100 million yuan, Zhang Yanjun has helped over 900 impoverished households in the surrounding villages and townships shake off poverty, with 76 of them earning an annual income of over 100,000 yuan.

In December 2017, Zhang Yanjun was honored to be one of the Top Ten Poverty Alleviation Figures in Henan.

01

02

01 张艳军（右二）和菇农一起规划壮大食用菌基地规模。

02 张艳军（左二）和菇农观看现代农业食用菌基地规划图。

03 张艳军（中）向菇农讲解双孢菇种植技术。

01 Zhang Yanjun (second from right) and some farmers are planning on expanding the edible fungi base.

02 Zhang Yanjun (second from left) and some farmers examining the blueprint of the Modern Agriculture and Edible Fungi Base.

03 Zhang Yanjun (middle) talking with farmers about agricus bisporus planting techniques.

03

04

05

06

04 2018年1月7日，张艳军（右）在贫困户大棚里向菇农讲解双孢菇采摘技术要领。

05 张艳军帮扶的贫困户的大棚里又长出一茬双孢菇。

06 张艳军（左）在了解双孢菇市场行情。

04 January 7, 2018. Zhang Yanjun (right) explaining how to pick agricus bisporus in a greenhouse.

05 Agricus bisporus in a greenhouse.

06 Zhang Yanjun (left) doing market research.

07 菇农在大棚里采摘双孢菇。
08 张艳军当选为2017河南十大年度扶贫人物。

07 A farmer picking agricus bisporus in a greenhouse.
08 Zhang Yanjun being honored as one of the Top Ten Poverty Alleviation Figures in Henan in 2017.

07

08

组织实施好易地扶贫搬迁工程，确保搬迁群众住房安全得到保障，饮水安全、出行、用电等基本生活条件得到明显改善，享有便利可及的教育、医疗等基本公共服务，迁出区生态环境得到有效治理，确保有劳动能力的贫困家庭后续发展有门路、转移就业有渠道、收入水平不断提高，实现建档立卡搬迁人口搬得出、稳得住、能脱贫。

——《“十三五”脱贫攻坚规划》

We must ensure that poverty alleviation through relocation projects will be well implemented so that those who relocate will be entitled to substantially improved housing, drinking water safety, transportation, electricity access and other basic living conditions, that they enjoy easily accessible education, health care and other basic public services, and that the ecological environment of their original residences will be well managed. We must also ensure that after relocation, impoverished families with ability to work will have ways to make a living, access to employment and earn growing incomes in their new place of residence. Registered impoverished people shall be relocated where they are able to live a stable life and shake off poverty.

——*National Plan for Poverty Alleviation During the 13th Five-Year Plan Period (2016-2020)*

树挪死　人挪活

易地搬迁脱贫

Alleviating Poverty by Relocating Impoverished Population

惠水搬迁民众集体过大年

Relocated People in Guizhou's Huishui County Celebrate Chinese New Year Together

图/文　贺俊怡

Photos and Text by He Junyi

2017年1月22日，贵州省惠水县经济开发区明田移民新区传来山歌声和欢呼声。在新春佳节到来之际，住进新房子的上千名民众自发组织举行以“迁新家、过新年、谢党恩、恋乡愁”为主题的集体过大年活动。

惠水县明田易地扶贫搬迁安置点位于惠水县经济开发区内。该县依托园区企业多、就业空间大等优势，规划建设园区产业型安置点，全部建成后，计划集中安置全县80%以上的搬迁对象。

On January 22, 2017, folk songs and cheers could be heard from the Mingtian New District in Huishui County's Economic Development Zone in Guizhou Province. With the advent of the Chinese New Year, thousands of people who had moved into new houses spontaneously organized a collective Chinese New Year gala. When fully completed, this relocation site will be able to accommodate over 80% of the relocated people in the county.

01 民众在移民服务中心张贴对联。
02 民众在新家阳台上欣赏小区的环境。

01 Posting Chinese New Year couplets on the door frames of the Relocation Service Center.
02 New building of the relocated.

01

02

03

04

03 苗族群众载歌载舞庆祝乔迁。

04 苗族妇女手拿着福字在新居前留影。

03 Miao folks celebrating their relocation.

04 A Miao woman holding the Chinese character “happiness” in front of her new home.

05

06

05 民众进行亲情接力趣味活动。
06 布依族妇女进行绣织比赛。

05 Family fun time.
06 Bouyei women having an embroidery competition.

07

08

07 布依族妇女在打糍粑。

08 布依族妇女用颜料在簸箕描画“新春快乐”几个大字。

07 Bouyei women making *ciba* (glutinous rice cake).

08 Painting Chinese characters “Happy Chinese Near Year.”

09

09 乔迁的民众喜笑颜开。
10 乔迁的民众举杯过大年。

09 Relocated people.
10 Relocated people celebrating Chinese New Year.

10

偏岩子新村　宜居美观“产村一体”

Pianyanzi New Village, Home and Employment in One Place

图/文　邱海鹰
Photos and Text by Qiu Haiying

四川省华蓥市阳和镇偏岩子新村一期工程是2014年年底完成的地质灾害避险搬迁安置点，33户地质灾害避险搬迁户，从山上地质灾害隐患区搬至山下新居。2016年春，当地又实施了供易地扶贫搬迁户和地质灾害避险搬迁户居住的二期工程，目前整个工程已全面竣工。

偏岩子新村按照环保、宜居、美观、经济等要求和中式明清风格连体别墅设计兴建，不仅体现了生态和谐，自然古朴的特色，还实现了“产村一体”的建设理念。新村既是乡村旅游载体，周围又有葡萄、柑橘等种植养殖产业基地，拓宽了搬迁贫困户的增收渠道。

The first phase of the Pianyanzi New Village was completed towards the end of 2014 to meet the relocation needs for purpose of geological risk avoidance. Thanks to that, 33 households were able to move away from the geological hazard zone up in the mountain to their new houses below. In 2016, the second phase was completed. By now, the entire project has been completed.

The Pianyanzi New Village are Chinese style townhouses designed to be environmentally-friendly, comfortable, elegant and economical, with features of ecological harmony, naturalness, and quaintness. In addition, they reflect the building concept of “integrating industrial enterprises into village life.” The new village features tourism and serves as bases of fruit production and animal husbandry, which ensure income growth for the relocated impoverished households.

01

02

01 2015年2月23日航拍偏岩子新村。

02 2015年1月13日，搬迁户在新居张贴春联和“福”字，喜迎新春佳节。

01 Aerial view of the Pianyanzi New Village, February 23, 2015.

02 January 13, 2015. Posting Chinese New Year couplets and “happiness” posters for their new house to celebrate the upcoming Chinese New Year.

03

03 2015年1月13日，搬迁户在新居门口享受冬日暖阳。
04 2017年9月6日，偏岩子新村居民在跳健身舞。

03 On January 13, 2015, three relocated women bathing in the warm winter sun.
04 Residents of Pianyanzi New Village exercising, September 6, 2017.

04

05

06

07

05 2017年9月6日，村民在新村旁的葡萄园采摘葡萄。
06 偏岩子新村二期工程一角。
07 偏岩子新村全貌。

05 A villager picking grapes in the grape plantation next to her residence, September 6, 2017.
06 Pianyanzi New Village, Phase II.
07 A panorama of Pianyanzi New Village.

喜迁“仫佬家园”
A New Ethnic Mulam Homestead

图/文　蒙增师（图02、04、07、08），韦如代（图01、03、05、06、09、10）
Photos and Text by Meng Zengshi (Photos 02, 04, 07 and 08) and Wei Rudai (Photos 01, 03, 05, 06, 09 and 10)

2017年11月28日，广西河池市罗城仫佬族自治县举行易地扶贫搬迁“仫佬家园”安置点千人集中搬迁入住新居仪式，420户1800多名贫困群众搬进新居。

“十三五”期间，罗城计划投资8.2亿元搬迁建档立卡户3187户13680人。该县采取集中安置为主、分散安置为辅的方式，在城区和乡镇选择区位优势明显、地形条件良好、适合搬迁户生存发展的一类土地作为安置点建设用地，“仫佬家园”就是其中一个较为集中的安置点。对在城区安置的贫困户，每户可享受由政府投资建设的1亩经济作物项目的10年利润分红，或者每户安排1间商铺门面，由政府代付租金5年；利用安置小区内的电子厂、周边企业和环卫公益岗等安排就业，或通过技能培训安排劳务输出，确保搬迁户每户有1人有相对稳定的就业岗位，让搬迁群众搬得出、住得下、可发展、能致富。

On November 28, 2017, over 1,800 relocated impoverished residents from 420 households collectively moved into their new homes at Mulam Homestead in Luocheng Mulam Autonomous County, Hechi City, Guangxi.

During the 13th Five-Year Plan period, Luocheng County plans to invest 820 million yuan to relocate 13,680 documented poor from a total of 3,187 households. The Mulam Homestead is a relatively concentrated urban relocation site with favorable geographical and topographic features that promise greater potential for making a better living. Each household relocated in the urban area is entitled to ten years' share of dividend from one *mu* (around 667 square meters) of government-invested cash crops. Alternatively, each household is provided with a shopfront with five years' rent paid by the government. The relocated residents can also be employed by an electronics factory within the community, by surrounding companies or public service departments such as maintenance and sanitation. They can also choose to work away from their home village after receiving relevant job skill training. The idea is that each of the relocated households will have at least one member who is steadily employed. In sum, the relocated must be able to settle down and live a better life.

01

02

01 “仫佬家园”安置小区大门。

02 “仫佬家园”位于罗城仫佬族自治县黄金地段成龙湖公园周边，占地总面积443亩。

01 Entrance to the Mulam Homestead.

02 The Mulam Homestead has a total area of 443 *mu* (around 29.5 hectares) and is favorably located in the perimeters of Lake Chenglong Park in Luocheng Mulam Autonomous County.

03

04

03 “仫佬家园”一角。
04 东门镇中石村贫困群众整理衣物准备搬入“仫佬家园”。

03 A corner of the Mulam Homestead.
04 Ready to move in their new home.

05 东门镇龙山村朱朝屯搬迁户龙善学一家把行李装车运往新居。
06 移民搬迁车队驶向“么佬家园”。

05 Long Shanxue and his family are loading the truck with packaged furniture, ready to move from Longshan Village, Dongmen Town to their new residence.
06 Relocation buses going to the Mulam Homestead.

05

06

07

08

07 贫困群众胸带红花抵达“仫佬家园”参加入住仪式。

08 仫佬族贫困群众抱着新居钥匙开心地笑了。

07 Going to a relocation ceremony at the Mulam Homestead.

08 The key to the new home.

09

10

09 搬迁户龙善学一家搬运行李进入新居。
10 搬迁户龙善学一家搬进新居。

09 Long Shanxue and his family moving in.
10 Long Shanxue and a family member moving furniture into their new home.

黄土高坡移民住新村
Villagers on the Loess Plateau Move into New Houses

图/文　袁宏彦
Photos and Text by Yuan Hongyan

2017年8月，位于宁夏银川市金凤区丰登镇润丰村的移民安置点，白墙黛瓦，道路宽阔，绿意盎然。宁夏西吉县白崖乡半子沟村的首批138户577人告别自然环境恶劣、干旱少雨的黄土高坡，移民到省会银川市金凤区润丰村。

半子沟村地处宁夏南部山区，是集中连片特困地区，一方水土养活不了一方人，唯有易地搬迁才能实现脱贫致富。润丰村出门就是柏油路，进门就有水电气，屋内厨房、卫生间、客厅和卧室布局合理，自来水、暖气、天然气、有线电视等安装到位，每个卧室都配有床、柜子等家具，村民拎包就可入住。润丰村将分批安置半子沟村317户1300余人，规划建设平层住宅3.2万平方米，配套建设幼儿园、村部、卫生室等公共设施3300平方米，产业用地1400亩。

August 2017. Houses with white walls and black tiles, broad roads and verdant trees – this is a relocation site in Runfeng Village, Fengdeng Town, Yinchuan City, Ningxia. The relocated were 557 people from 138 households of Banzigou Village, Baiya Township, Xiji County, who had just left the harsh natural environment of arid loess plateau and migrated to the aforesaid village.

Banzigou Village is situated in an extremely poor mountain area in southern Ningxia where people can barely make a living. The only way out is emigration to a better place. Runfeng Village has all the conveniences of asphalt roads, easy access to utilities, well-furnished houses complete with tap water, heating, natural gas and cable TV. Emigrants can literally move in with nothing more than their own luggage. Runfeng Village will accommodate more than 1,300 people from 317 households of Banzigou Village. Bungalows totaling 32,000 square meters and supporting public facilities, including a kindergarten, a village office building, and a clinic, totaling 3,300 square meters, will be built. In addition, 1,400 *mu* (around 93 hectares) of land will be allocated for industrial use.

01

02

03

01 润丰村移民安置点。
02 一户村民入住润丰村新居。
03 润丰村移民安置点里，一个小朋友正在擦拭新家的大门。

01 Runfeng Village's relocation site.
02 A family has just moved into their new home in Runfeng Village.
03 A boy cleaning up his new home.

04

04 村民在润丰村新居前聊天。
05 润丰村村民在宽阔的马路上散步。

04 New residents chatting in Runfeng Village.
05 Strolling on a broad road in Runfeng Village.

05

06

07

06 小朋友在润丰村里玩耍。
07 小朋友在润丰村文体中心打篮球。
08 润丰村新建幼儿园的老师精心收拾，准备迎接学生的到来。

06 Kids playing in the neighborhood.
07 Playing basketball at the cultural and sports center.
08 A newly-built kindergarten ready to open.

08

以提高贫困人口基本文化素质和贫困家庭劳动力技能为抓手，瞄准教育最薄弱领域，阻断贫困的代际传递。到2020年，贫困地区基础教育能力明显增强，职业教育体系更加完善，高等教育服务能力明显提升，教育总体质量显著提高，基本公共教育服务水平接近全国平均水平。

——《"十三五"脱贫攻坚规划》

We must concentrate on improving the basic literacy of the impoverished population and the laboring skills of impoverished households, target the weakest areas of education and cut out intergenerational transmission of poverty. By 2020, basic education conditions in poverty-stricken areas must be substantially improved; vocational education system further upgraded; higher education services and overall education quality promoted manifestly; and basic public education services brought close to the national average level.

——*National Plan for Poverty Alleviation During the 13th Five-Year Plan Period (2016-2020)*

阻断贫困的“遗传”

教育扶贫

Eradicating “Hereditary” Poverty Through Education

背篼图书馆
“Library on Shoulders”

图/文　张广玉
Photos and Text by Zhang Guangyu

2016年10月22日，云南省昭通市大关县“背篼图书馆”走进了该县悦乐镇新寨村海坝苗寨。

大关县位于乌蒙山腹地，一些村子不通公路，山路陡峻，有的路段连马儿都很难行走。为了确保贫困偏远山区群众和留守儿童享受文化惠民成果，大关县文化体育广播电视和旅游局开展文化扶贫，于2016年成立“背篼图书馆”送书服务工作队，开展巡回送书服务。工作队成员翻山越岭，将图书背到山里，把图书馆办到了农民家门口，为深山里的群众送去精神文化食粮，同时，还组织留守儿童开展作文竞赛、游戏、演出、讲故事等活动。至2018年年初，大关县已建成玉碗镇何家坡、阴山林口、团结，悦乐镇海坝、堡山、太阳坝，上高桥乡大麻窝，高桥镇罗汉林和天星镇龙塘等共11个“背篼图书馆”。

有图书，有阅读者，无论是什么地方都可以成为图书馆。

On October 22, 2016, a “Library on Shoulders” was manually “carried” from the county seat of Daguan, Zhaotong City, Yunnan Province into the Haiba Miao Village in Yuele Town.

Some of the villages of Daguan County located in the heart of the perilous Wumeng Mountains have no access to highways and the mountain paths there are so narrow that even horses have difficulty passing through. To make sure that the people and especially the left-behind children in the remote and impoverished mountain areas can benefit from the county’s cultural programs, the Daguan Culture, Sports, Radio and Tourism Bureau launched in 2016 a cultural campaign to alleviate poverty by setting up an itinerant “Library on Shoulders” book delivery service team. Service team members crossed over mountains to bring books to farmers’ homes. They also organized a series of cultural activities for left-behind children, including writing competitions, game play, performances, story-telling. By early 2018, Daguan County had built a total of 11 “Libraries on Shoulders” in places including Hejiapo Village, Yinshan Village, Linkou Village and Tuanjie Village in Yuwan Town; Haiba Village, Baoshan Village and Taiyangba Village in Yuele Town; Damawo Village in Shanggaoqiao Township; Luohanlin Village in Gaoqiao Town; and Longtang Village in Tianxing Town.

Wherever books and readers are, there libraries would be.

01 "背篼图书馆"工作队走4个多小时的山路前往海坝苗寨。
02 工作队在进入海坝苗寨的路途中负重爬山。

01 Libraries on the move. Service team members need to walk more than four hours to reach Haiba Miao Village.
02 On the way to Haiba Miao Village.

01

02

03

03 当地群众用隆重的苗族礼节迎接工作队。
04 工作队在海坝苗寨开展送书服务。

03 Welcome ceremony.
04 Books being read on delivery.

04

05

06

05 工作队成员向孩子们赠送学习用品。

06 海坝苗寨的孩子们被图书深深吸引。

05 A kid receiving free stationery from a service team member.

06 Thirst for knowledge.

07

08

07 “背篼图书馆”工作队成员与海坝苗寨的孩子一起阅读。

08 “背篼图书馆”向当地赠送了图书柜和400余册图书。

07 A “Library on Shoulders” service team member in a reading session with kids.

08 “Library on Shoulders” donated a bookshelf and over 400 books to these kids.

09

10

09 海坝苗寨的孩子们在临时图书馆内读书。
10 "背篼图书馆"工作队完成任务离开时，海坝苗寨的村民依依不舍，挥手告别。

09 Kids reading in the temporary library.
10 Saying goodbye to the book deliverers.

“红蜡烛”点亮贫困儿童心灵
“Red Candle” Shedding Light to Impoverished Children

图/文 章轲
Photos and Text by Zhang Ke

2007年，“红蜡烛助教计划”由国泰基金发起，每年开展支学助教活动，致力于改变贫困地区的教学环境和学习条件。该计划以授之于渔、互助分享、回馈社会、创造希望为理念，扶贫助优，同时帮助当地教师，推动中国贫困地区教育事业发展。

以扶和助为主，奖为辅；以实物、资金、辅导行动为主；以内为主，内外结合；“红蜡烛”通过提供交流、分享、互助的平台，结集富含公益之心的各界人士共同推进此项教育公益事业。

截至2017年，“红蜡烛助教计划”在国内完成助教28次，捐助“红蜡烛图书馆”12座及“红蜡烛·梦想中心”多媒体教室6个，助养学生228人，捐赠图书2.2万本，受益师生8500多名。

The “Red Candle Teaching Assistance Plan” initiated by China’s Guotai Fund in 2007 provides teaching assistance to rural areas every year as part of its commitment to change the teaching and learning environment in impoverished areas. The plan aims at assisting local teachers and promoting educational development in China’s poverty-stricken areas.

The plan provides support as well as reward, in cash or real terms or guidance and summons philanthropic people from all circles at home and abroad to jointly promote this philanthropic cause in education and establish a platform for exchange, sharing and mutual assistance.

As of 2017, the plan had completed 28 teaching assistance missions, donated 12 “Red Candle Libraries,” six “Red Candle Dream” multimedia classrooms, 22,000 books, and financially supported 228 students, benefitting more than 8,500 teachers and students.

01 2012年9月11日，甘肃省甘南藏族自治州迭部县，33名益哇乡小学的"三好学生"领到了"红蜡烛助教计划"的奖学金。

02 扎尕那小学学生康主草获得了国泰基金提供的奖学金。

01 On September 11, 2012, 33 honor students from Yiwa Township Elementary School (located in Tewo County, Gannan Tibetan Autonomous Prefecture, Gansu Province) received "Red Candle Teaching Assistance Plan" scholarships.

02 A student from Zhagana Elementary School received a scholarship from Guotai Fund.

01

02

03

04

03 志愿者给学生们讲课。
04 志愿者给学生们上音乐课。

03 Volunteer teachers at work.
04 A volunteer teacher giving a music lesson.

05

06

05 “红蜡烛助教计划” 走进益哇乡小学。
06 志愿者和学生们开展拔河比赛。

05 “Red Candle Teaching Assistance Plan” sponsoring programs at Yiwa Township Elementary School.
06 A tug of war between volunteer teachers and the students.

07

08

09

07 益哇乡的小学生们表演节目。
08 益哇乡的小学生与志愿者互动，欢乐满满。
09 益哇乡打出"知识改变命运　教育决定未来"的标语。

07 Students giving a performance.
08 Elementary school students in Yiwa Township having fun with volunteers.
09 A slogan that says "knowledge changes fate and education determines future."

教师夫妻坚守穷乡村34载
A Couple Who Have Been Teaching in a Poor Village for 34 Years

图/文　钟敏
Photos and Text by Zhong Min

2017年9月6日，四川省遂宁市射洪县天仙镇双庙教学点的师生迎来他们平常的一天。

双庙以前是射洪县最北端偏远的一个乡，1992年撤乡建镇后，之前有近千名学生的天仙镇双庙学校，变成只有两个班、7个学生的双庙教学点。为了让这里的孩子能顺利上学读书，黄小林和严云春这对乡村教师夫妻坚守这个学校34年，在平凡的工作岗位上，立志为家乡的教育事业做奉献，尽最大努力培养更多有用人才，改变家乡的落后面貌。

2015年3月，由中国名师联盟携手中国青少年发展基金会共同发起的中国名师联盟·希望工程园丁奖揭晓。黄小林老师荣获“2014中国名师联盟·希望工程园丁奖”。这个奖项旨在表彰奖励在农村贫困地区基础教育事业中做出突出成绩的优秀乡村教师，弘扬人民教师献身教育事业的崇高精神，倡导尊师重教、关心支持农村贫困地区基础教育发展的社会风尚。

On September 6, 2017, teachers and students at Shuangmiao Learning Center in Tianxian Town, Shehong County, Sichuan Province, started their day as usual.

Shuangmiao is a town in the northernmost part of Shehong County. In 1992, the Shuangmiao School with close to a thousand students was downsized into Shuangmiao Learning Center with only seven students in two classes. To enable the students to go to school as usual, Huang Xiaolin and Yan Yunchun chose to stay on at Shungmiao. Their 34 years of commitment to the cause of education and poverty reduction in their hometown is phenomenal.

In March 2015, Huang Xiaolin became winner of the award which was co-sponsored by the Chinese League of Best Mentors and the China Youth Development Foundation to honor rural elementary school teachers for their outstanding contribution to primary education in impoverished rural areas.

01

02

01 黄小林为双庙教学点三年级学生上课。
02 黄小林辅导学生做功课。

01 Huang Xiaolin teaching three third graders at Shuangmiao Learning Center.
02 Teaching spelling by hand.

03

03 严云春辅导幼儿班的孩子学数学知识。
04 严云春辅导幼儿班的孩子学算术。
05 一个幼儿班的孩子正在掰手指头做算术题。
06 孩子们在体育课上玩黄小林捡回来的废旧汽车轮胎。

03 Yan Yunchun teaching arithmetic to a preschooler.
04 Teaching the basics.
05 A schoolboy doing finger counting.
06 Playing with used tires collected by Huang Xiaolin.

04

05

06

07

07 孩子们在体育课上踢破旧的足球。
08 孩子们在教室里吃午餐。

07 A worn soccer ball for PE.
08 Having lunch in the classroom.

08

09

09 黄小林和严云春与孩子们一起升国旗。

09 Huang Xiaolin, Yan Yunchun and students at a national flag raising ceremony.

花季少女复学记
A Teenage School Girl Returns to School

图/文　饶国君
Photos and Text by Rao Guojun

2016年2月24日，重庆市云阳职业教育中心“旅游服务与管理”专业2016级2班，年仅14岁、失学1年多的花季少女周琼坐进教室，开始重返校园的第一堂课。

周琼的家位于云阳县耀灵镇鸣凤村7组，一家共6口人，父母长期患病，奶奶年逾八旬，19岁和17岁的两个哥哥均外出务工。由于家境困难，周琼读到初二便辍学在家，帮助父母做农活。

在扶贫攻坚结对过程中，云阳县人民法院派驻工作组进村，把周昌银一家的帮扶脱贫工作落实下来。征求其父母的意见后，帮扶工作组决定让周琼重返课堂。工作组为周琼联系了插班班级，采取措施弥补初中未竟课程，并号召干警捐资补贴其生活费用；学校也根据周琼的实际情况，全免书费学费，失学一年有余的花季少女终于回到课堂。

On February 24, 2016, Zhou Qiong, a 14-year-old girl who majored in tourism service and management at Chongqing's Yunyang Vocational Education Center, returned to school after dropping out for over a year.

Zhou Qiong comes from a family of six in Mingfeng Village, Yaoling Town, Yunyang County, Chongqing. Her parents suffer from chronic illnesses; her grandma is in her 80s; and her two elder brothers are migrant workers. Due to poverty, Zhou Qiong dropped out of school by second grade in junior middle school to help her parents with farm work.

During a campaign of targeted poverty alleviation, a work team dispatched by Yunyang County People's Court to the village decided to help Zhou Qiong out. They called for donations on her behalf and contacted her school for tuition and fee waiver and other remedial measures. Zhou was ultimately able to return to school.

01 失学以来，周琼就待在家里做家务、干农活。
02 返校前的早晨，周琼与前来接她入学的干警刘媛在田野间跑步。

01 After quitting school, Zhou Qiong helped her parents with housework and farming.
02 On the morning of returning to school, Zhou Qiong and Liu Yuan, an officer who came to pick her up, were running in the field.

01

02

03

04

03 干警刘媛为周琼梳头。
04 周琼的家是用泥砖和木头砌成的小楼。
05 周琼的母亲谭扬清（右一）一早为女儿煮汤圆送行。
06 周琼美美地吃上了一碗汤圆。

03 Liu Yuan doing Zhou Qiong's hair.
04 Zhou Qiong's house is built with clay bricks and wood.
05 Zhou Qiong's mother Tan Yangqing (right) making breakfast before sending her daughter back to school.
06 A breakfast of sweet dumplings.

05

06

07

08

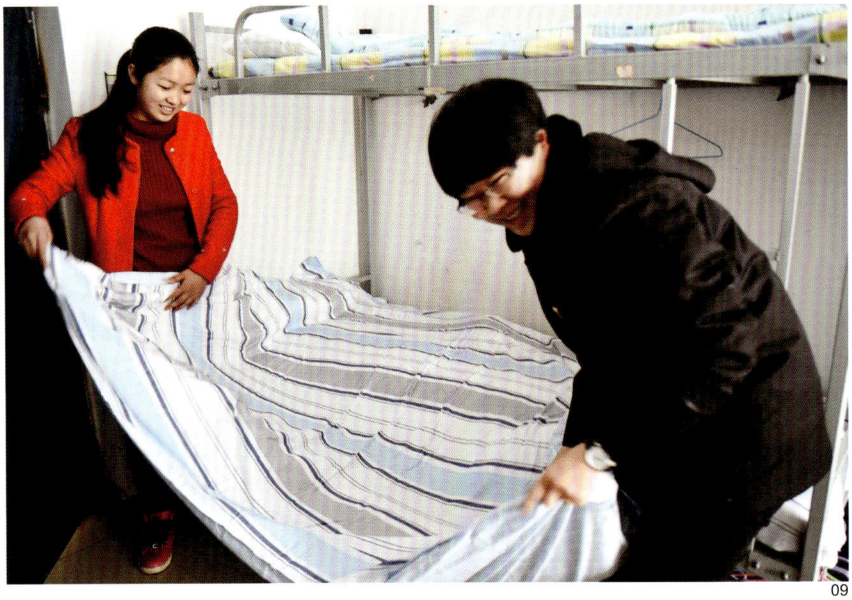
09

07 一切准备妥当，周琼出发返校。
08 周琼在父亲周昌银的陪伴下，走进学校。
09 周琼入住学生宿舍。

07 Off to go.
08 Zhou Qiong and her father Zhou Changyin on campus.
09 Making bed in dorm.

10

10 周琼（中）在课堂上观看视频“入学第一课”。

10 First class after return.

改善贫困地区医疗卫生机构条件，提升服务能力，缩小区域间卫生资源配置差距，基本医疗保障制度进一步完善，建档立卡贫困人口大病和慢性病得到及时有效救治，就医费用个人负担大幅减轻，重大传染病和地方病得到有效控制，基本公共卫生服务实现均等化，因病致贫返贫问题得到有效解决。

——《“十三五”脱贫攻坚规划》

We must improve the conditions of medical and health service institutions in impoverished regions, strengthen service capabilities and narrow the gap in health resource allocation. We will further improve the primary medical care insurance system; ensure that serious and chronic diseases of documented impoverished poor get timely and effective treatment, that patients' out of pocket medical expenses are reduced substantially, that major infectious diseases get effectively controlled; that essential public health services are equally shared; and that illness-caused poverty issues get resolved effectively.

——National Plan for Poverty Alleviation During the 13th Five-Year Plan Period (2016-2020)

应对因病致贫　救助在行动

健康扶贫

Relieving Poverty Caused by Illnesses

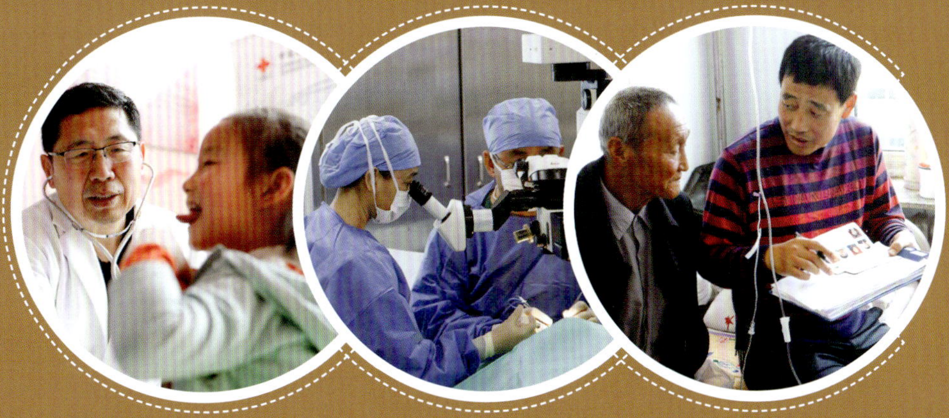

“天使之旅”愈合天使的心
“Angels’ Journey” Heals Little Angels

图/文　刘关关
Photos and Text by Liu Guanguan

先天性心脏病是胚胎期心脏血管发育异常而造成的畸形性疾病，发病率约占出生活婴儿的0.7%～0.8%。就我国目前的医疗技术水平，99%的患儿是可以通过手术治疗得到康复的。但许多贫困家庭承担不起上万元的医疗费用，往往只能放弃治疗。

2006年5月，为救助贫困家庭的先天性心脏病儿童，中国红十字基金会倡导设立专项公益基金——“天使阳光基金”，该基金成为中国红基会“红十字天使计划”的重要组成部分。

2011年起，中国红基会邀请三甲医院知名医疗专家，发起“天使之旅”先心病筛查活动，赴贫困偏远地区进行筛查及救治。2017年还启动了“天使之旅——‘一带一路’人道救助计划”，救助了阿富汗、蒙古国先心病患儿。2018年，基金计划走进甘肃、四川、云南、广西等更多边远贫困地区，积极拉动社会资源，减轻贫困先心病患儿手术治疗的经济压力，同时期盼更多人关注先心病儿童群体，为患儿带去福音。

Congenital heart disease (CHD) is a deformity caused by cardiovascular dysplasia during the embryonic period. Morbidity among born live infants is between 0.7% and 0.8%. With current medical technology, 99% of CHD afflicted children in China can be cured through operation. However, many impoverished families cannot afford medical expenses that can add up to 10,000 yuan per operation and often give up treatment.

To help poverty-stricken families with CHD afflicted children, the Chinese Red Cross Foundation established a special philanthropic fund called “Angel and Sunshine Fund” in May 2006, which became an important part of the Foundation’s “Red Cross Angel Program.”

Since 2011, the Foundation has been inviting well-known medical experts from top hospitals to join in “Angels’ Journey” CHD screening campaigns to screen and treat patients in remote and impoverished areas. In 2017, it launched the “Angels’ Journey: Belt and Road Humanitarian Aid Plan” to treat CHD afflicted children in Afghanistan and Mongolia. In 2018, the Plan made its way to Gansu, Sichuan, Yunnan, Guangxi and many other remote and impoverished areas to proactively mobilize social resources to relieve the economic burden of operational expenses on poor families with CHD afflicted children and to call for more concern and care for such patients.

01

01 2016年，“天使之旅——贵州贫困先心病儿童筛查行动”在贵阳市修文县启动，两位儿童跟随家长参加仪式。

02 “天使之旅——贵州贫困先心病儿童筛查行动”现场。

01 In 2016, “Angels’ Journey: Screening for CHD Afflicted Children in Guizhou” was launched in Xiuwen County, Guiyang City. Two children came to attend this event with their parents.

02 Screening for CHD afflicted children in Guizhou.

02

03

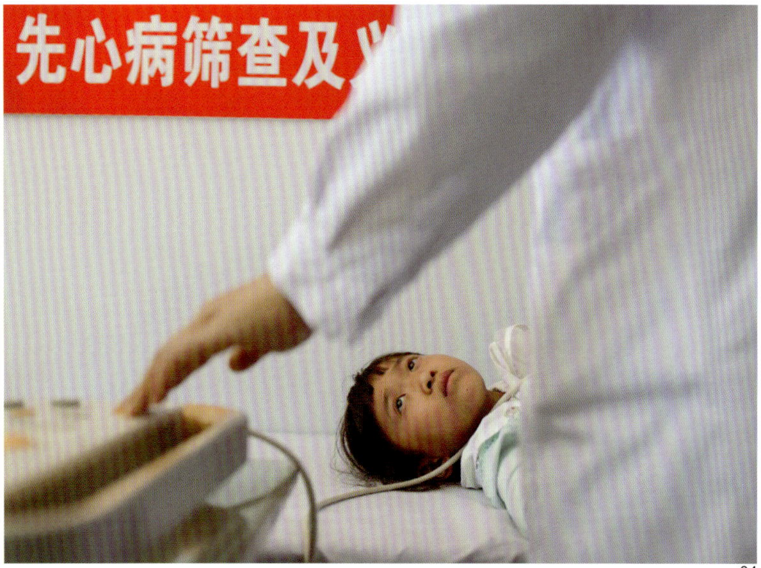

04

03 2016年，“天使之旅——走进大兴安岭”一行在加格达奇区第四小学进行先心病儿童筛查和义诊。符合手术指征的患儿将赴牡丹江市接受免费手术治疗。

04 一名儿童在“天使之旅——走进大兴安岭”活动中接受筛查和义诊。

03 Free CHD screening and diagnosis for children at Jagdaqi No. 4 Elementary School, 2016. Patients who needed operation would receive free operation in Mudanjiang City.

04 A child receiving free screening and diagnosis during the “Angels’ Journey to Greater Hinggan Mountain.”

05

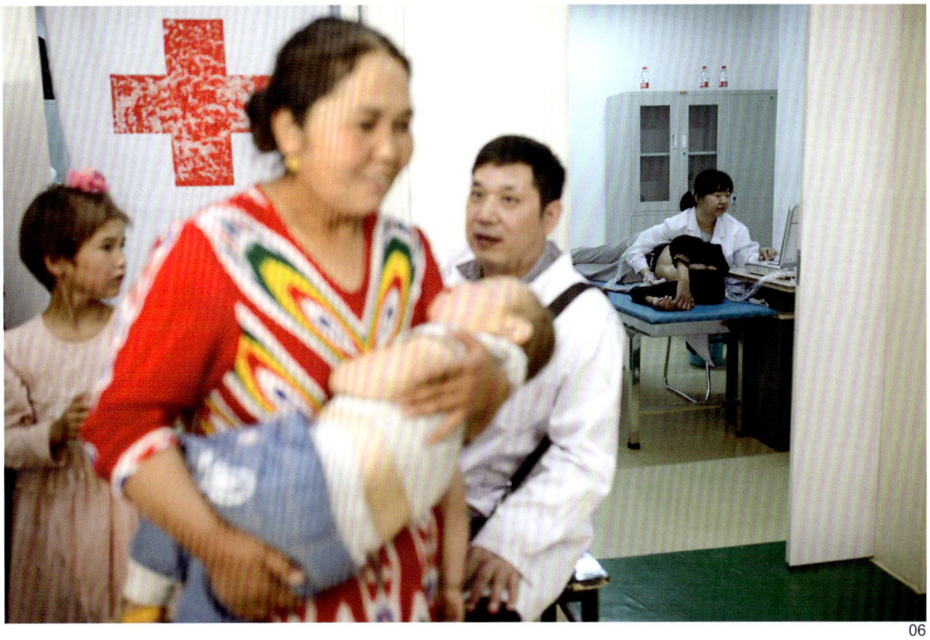

06

05 2017年，“天使明心基金成立暨‘一带一路’人道救助计划新疆先心病患儿筛查救助行动”在喀什展开，主要筛查对象为0—14岁儿童，考虑到新疆南疆医疗资源匮乏，救助对象放宽至贫困家庭的成年先天性心脏病患者。

06 当地群众在“天使明心基金成立暨‘一带一路’人道救助计划新疆先心病患儿筛查救助行动”中接受义诊筛查。

05 Screening of CHD children and impoverished CHD adult patients in Kashgar, Xinjiang in 2017.

06 CHD afflicted children screening as part of the Belt and Road Humanitarian Aid Plan in Xinjiang.

07

08

09

07 2017年，经中国红十字援外医疗队专家筛查的第二批41名蒙古国先心病患儿乘坐列车抵达北京接受治疗。此前，“天使之旅——‘一带一路’大病患儿人道救助计划蒙古国行动”在乌兰巴托开展先心病患儿筛查，首批12名患儿在呼和浩特成功完成免费手术。

08 “天使之旅——‘一带一路’大病患儿人道救助计划蒙古国行动”中，中国红十字会副会长郭长江在清华大学第一附属医院看望蒙古国先心病患儿。

09 “天使之旅——‘一带一路’大病患儿人道救助计划蒙古国行动”中，蒙古国驻华大使冈呼雅格的夫人在北京安贞医院看望入院治疗的先心病患儿。

07 In 2017, the second batch of 41 CHD afflicted children from Mongolia arrived at Beijing Railway Station for treatment by Chinese experts organized by the Chinese Red Cross Foundation. The first batch of 12 Mongolian CHD patients had earlier received free successful operation in Hohhot.

08 During “Angels’ Journey to Mongolia,” Guo Changjiang, vice president of Chinese Red Cross Foundation, visits a Mongolian CHD afflicted child at First Hospital of Tsinghua University.

09 Mrs. Gankhuyag, wife of the Mongolian Ambassador in China, visits a CHD afflicted child being treated at Anzhen Hospital in Beijing.

10

11

10 2018年，“天使之旅——山东贫困先心病儿童救助行动”中，一名儿童在高密市妇幼保健院接受检查。

11 “天使之旅——山东贫困先心病儿童救助行动”中，一名儿童在诸城市妇幼保健院接受检查。

10 Screening a kid from an impoverished family at the Maternal and Child Health Care Center in Gaomi City, Shandong Province, in 2018.

11 A kid receiving a health examination at the Maternal and Child Health Care Center in Zhucheng City, Shandong Province.

“共铸中国心”把爱带到“老少边穷”地区
“Building Up Heart Health” in China’s Impoverished Areas

图/文　李重阳（图01-06、12-13），任海霞（图07-09），安源（图10-11）
Photos and Text by Li Chongyang (Photos 01-06 and 12-13), Ren Haixia (Photos 07-09) and An Yuan (Photos 10-11)

“共铸中国心”大型公益项目是首都医疗卫生界高端专家、爱心人士发起并参与的，以“老少边穷”地区心脑血管疾病救助救治和健康关爱为核心的大规模定点、定向的主题公益行动。2010年起，这一活动被纳入中央统战部“同心工程”，称为“同心·共铸中国心”工程。2008年至今，“同心·共铸中国心”的专家医疗团队和志愿者们持续为“老少边穷”地区人民群众开展医疗救助活动，内容涵盖了地方病调研、义诊巡诊、爱心捐赠、医疗培训、健康讲座、少儿先心病筛查及救助等，受救助的群众累计达百万人次，千余名先天性心脏病患儿得到免费手术，近千名白内障患者重见光明。

“Building Up Heart Health in China” is a large philanthropic program initiated by senior medical experts and philanthropists in Beijing, for the purpose of treating and caring for patients suffering from cardiovascular diseases in former revolutionary bases, border and underdeveloped areas as well as areas inhabited by ethnic minority groups (collectively known as “Four Targeted Poverty-Stricken Areas”). Since 2010, this program has been merged into the “One Heart Project” of the United Front Work Department of the CPC Central Committee. From 2008 up till today, the expert medical teams and volunteers of this project have provided medical assistance to people in the Four Targeted Poverty-Stricken Areas, in the form of endemic disease research, free and itinerant clinical diagnosis, philanthropic donations, medical training, health lectures and health screening and treatment of children’s CHD (congenital heart disease). A total of one million people have benefited from this program, more than a thousand CHD children have received free surgical treatment, and close to a thousand cataract patients have regained sight.

01

02

01 为保护高原骑行者的健康，提醒他们预防肺心病，共铸中国心“318”爱心诊室在理塘318国道旁揭幕。

02 “共铸中国心”组委会自2015年起推出“四个一”工程，即给藏区部分寺庙配备一间医务室、一间浴室、一间图书室和一间健身房。图为其中一间健身房。

01 To ensure the health of travelers on the plateau and caution them against the risk of lung and heart diseases, the “318 Loving Heart Clinic” of the “Building Up Heart Health in China” program was set up near the No. 318 National Highway in Litang County.

02 The “Building Up Heart Health in China” Organizing Committee has been implementing a “Four Rooms” Project since 2015, which is to build a clinic, a bathroom, a reading room and a fitness room for certain temples in Tibet. This is a fitness room.

03

04

03 “共铸中国心”组委会“四个一”工程中修建的图书室。

04 “共铸中国心”健康公益会诊平台“莲花会诊”在四川省甘孜藏族自治州揭牌，当地百姓可以通过该平台得到北京各医院专家的诊疗。

03 A reading room supported by the “Four Rooms” Project.

04 “Lotus Consultation,” a philanthropic health consultation platform sponsored by the “Building Up Heart Health in China” program, was set up in Garze Tibetan Autonomous Prefecture. Through this platform, locals can consult health experts from hospitals in Beijing.

05

05 “同心 · 共铸中国心”健康学院甘孜分院揭牌。为了给受援地培养一支不走的医疗队，“共铸中国心”组委会把搭建交流互动学习平台、培训当地基层医生作为重点。

06 “同心 · 共铸中国心”组委会牵手北京清华长庚医院、北京胸科医院和甘孜州合作，建立肝包虫、肺结核防治指导中心。肝包虫、肺结核这两大类传染疾病在甘孜藏族自治州有很高的发病率。

05 Grand opening of a health college in Garze sponsored by the “Building Up Heart Health in China” program. The idea is to train and establish a permanent medical team in the aided area.

06 The “Building Up Heart Health in China” Organizing Committee worked with the Beijing’s Tsinghua Changgeng Hospital, Beijing Chest Hospital and the government of Garze to build a service center for preventing hepatic hydatid and tuberculosis, two infectious diseases of high morbidity in Garze.

06

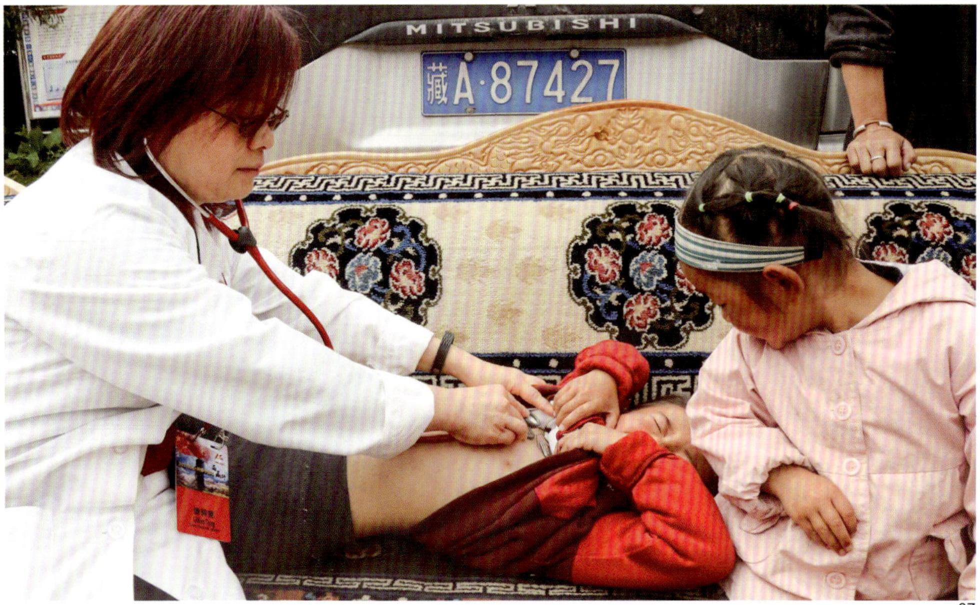

07

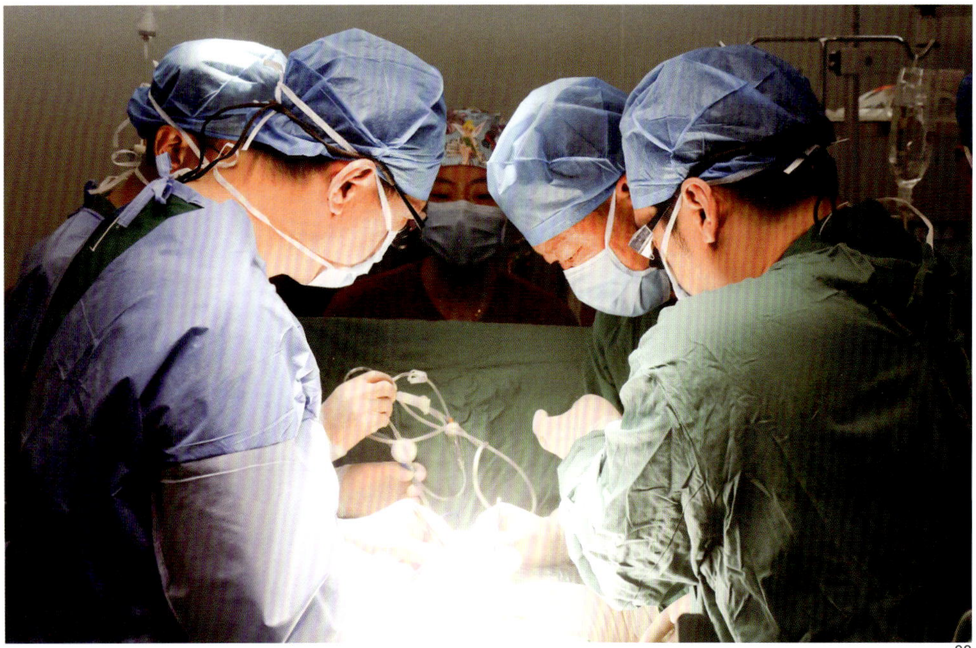

08

07 在2017“同心·共铸中国心”西藏行大型医疗公益活动中，医务工作者到西藏林芝巴宜区的八一镇多布村义诊。

08 在2017“同心·共铸中国心”西藏行活动中，来自北京的医学专家在林芝为当地包虫病患者进行手术救治。

07 A doctor checking on a young patient in Duobu Village, Bayi Town, Nyingchi City during a free medical service campaign in Tibet in 2017.

08 Medical experts from Beijing performing an operation for a patient in Tibet who was suffering from hydatid disease during an outreach in 2017.

09

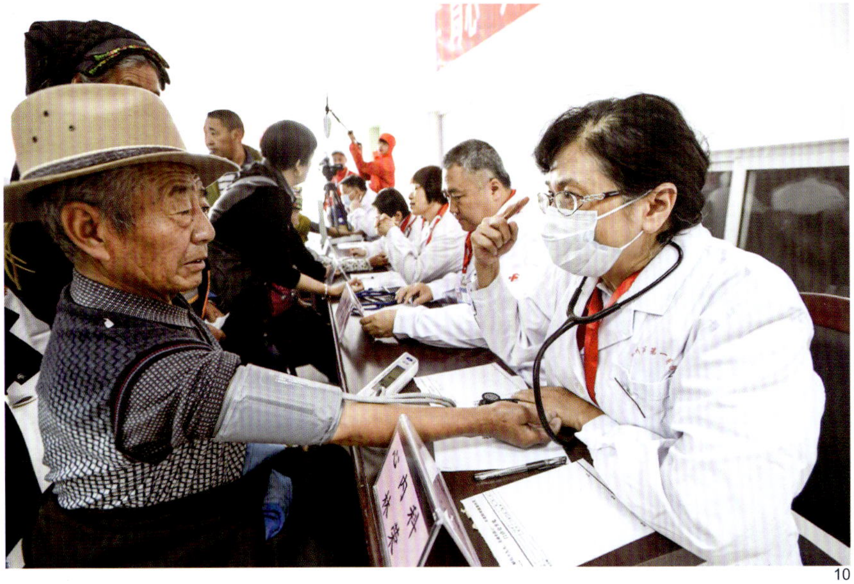

10

09 在2017“同心·共铸中国心”西藏行活动中，医学专家团队在林芝开展义诊并为患者免费发放药品。

10 参加2017“同心·共铸中国心”健康扶贫阿坝行公益活动的医疗卫生专家走进四川省阿坝州马尔康市开展医疗义诊活动。

09 A medical expert team providing free service and medicine to patients in Nyingchi in 2017.

10 Medical experts providing free service to patients in Barkam City, Aba Tibetan and Qiang Autonomous Prefecture, Sichuan Province in 2017.

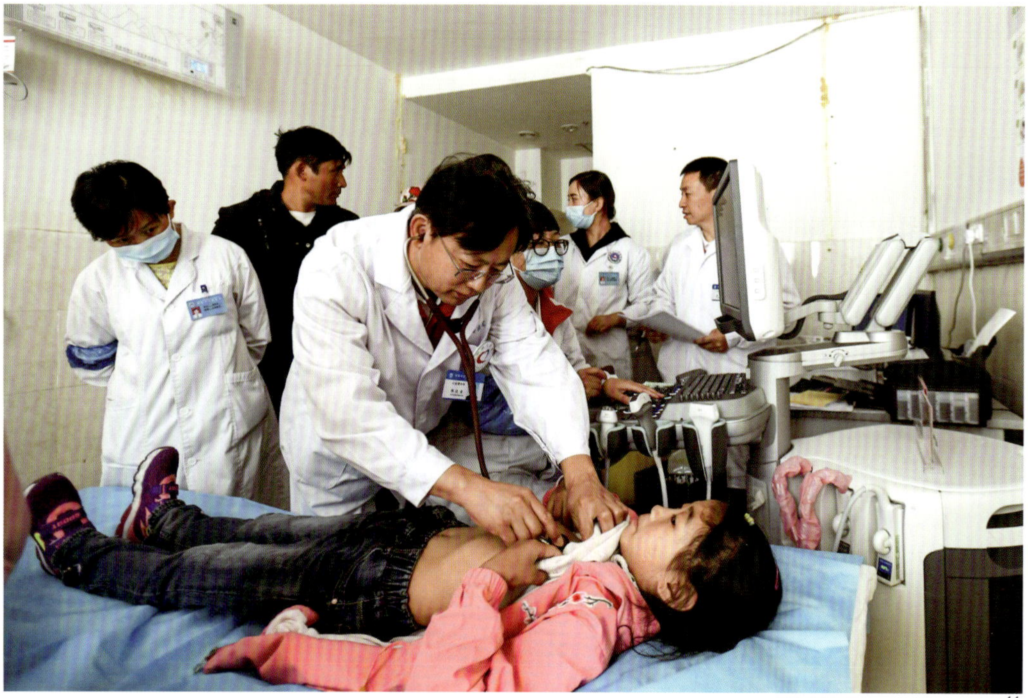
11

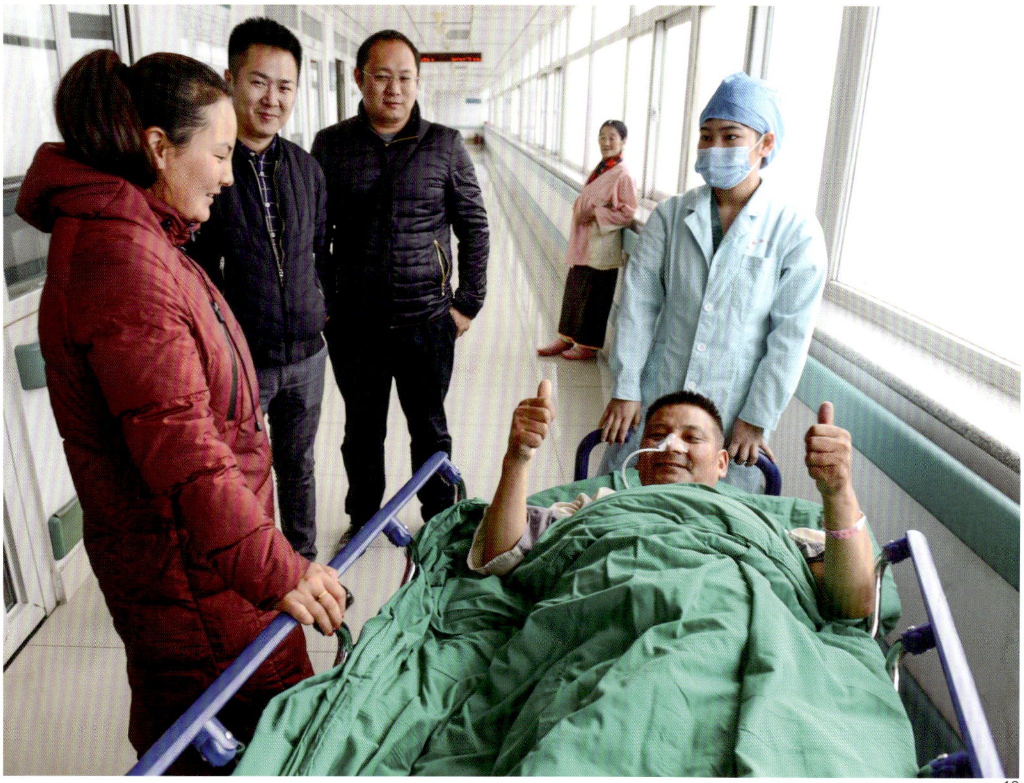
12

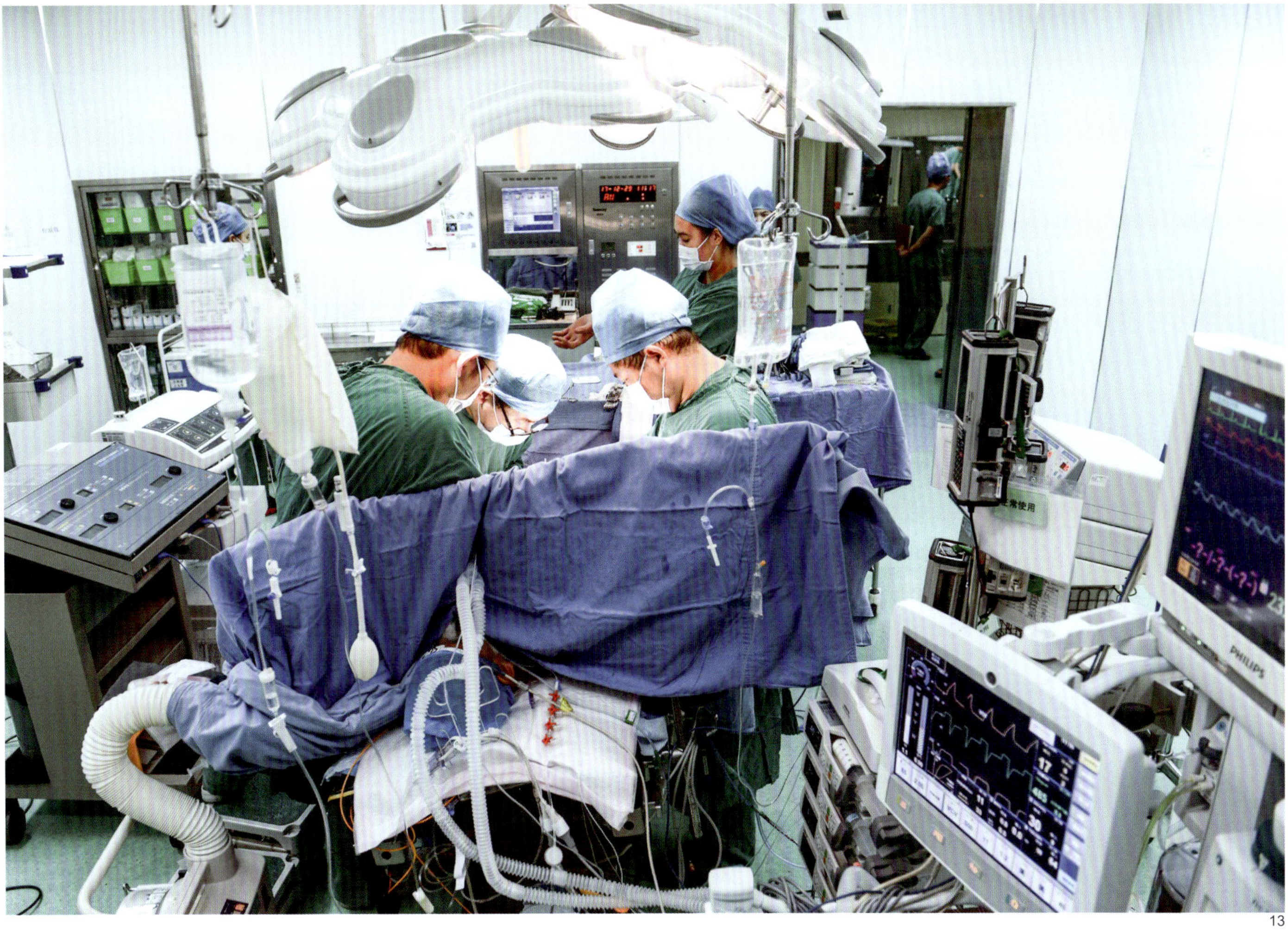

13

11 在2017“同心·共铸中国心”健康扶贫阿坝行公益活动中，医疗卫生专家在阿坝州医院进行少儿先心病筛查。
12 2017年年底，来自西藏林芝的达娃大叔被送到北京接受肝包虫切除手术。手术前他说：“放心，放心，我对手术有信心，我对医院有信心，我对医生有信心，手术一定能成功。”达娃大叔是“同心·共铸中国心”公益项目中一位受助患者。
13 2017年年底，由首都医科大学附属佑安医院李宁院长带领的顶尖专家手术团队，为达娃大叔实施肝包虫切除手术。

11 Medical experts screening children for CHD in Aba Prefectural Hospital, 2017.
12 In December 2017, Dawa from Nyingchi, Tibet was sent to Beijing to receive hepatic hydatid excision. He said before the operation, “Don’t worry. I’ll be fine. I believe the hospital and the doctors. The operation will be successful.” He was one of the beneficiaries of the “Building Up Heart Health in China” welfare program.
13 Top experts led by Li Ning, president of Beijing Youan Hospital, doing a hepatic hydatid excision procedure on Dawa, December 2017.

“健康快车”重燃贫困白内障患者生活之光
“Health Express” Gives Vision Back to Cataract Patients

图/文 张浩（图01-05）、张添福（图06）、石艺媛（图07-10）
Photos and Text by Zhang Hao (Photos 01-05), Zhang Tianfu (Photo 06) and Shi Yiyuan (Photos 07-10)

“健康快车”是中国唯一建在火车上的慈善眼科医院，是1997年7月1日香港回归祖国时，香港同胞送给内地同胞的礼物，旨在为偏远地区的贫困白内障患者提供免费手术治疗，让他们重见光明，摆脱因病致贫的困境。

在20年的发展中，健康快车由最初的1列火车医院增加到4列，扶助范围也扩展到国内眼科医疗的各个方面：培训欠发达地区的眼科医生；于偏远地区援建眼科中心；开展糖尿病视网膜病变（简称糖网病）筛查防治工作；推动国际眼科医师考试（ICO考试）在中国内地的普及；邀请海外眼科专家深入中国内地开展学术研讨与指导工作；设立奖学金鼓励优秀眼科医生赴国际顶尖医学院进修；为“一带一路”沿线国家提供国际慈善眼科医疗服务等。

在20年不懈的工作中，“健康快车火车医院”累计为超过19.2万名贫困白内障患者实施复明手术；建成了75所“健康快车眼科中心”，培训内地基层眼科医生2万多人次；建成40所糖网中心，累计筛查糖尿病患者近7.6万人，挽救其中濒临失明的糖网病患者2400多人。

“Health Express” is the only train-based charity eye hospital in China. This gift given by HKSAR to the mainland of China when Hong Kong returned on July 1, 1997 is used to provide free cataract removal surgeries to patients in remote and poverty-stricken areas so that they may regain their sight and free themselves from the bondage of poverty caused by illnesses.

Within 20 years, “Health Express” hospitals have grown in number from one to four. Aid activities have expanded to all aspects of ophthalmology, including the training of ophthalmologists in underdeveloped areas, the sponsoring of eye clinics in remote areas, diabetic retinopathy (DR) screening, promotion of the International Council of Ophthalmology (ICO) Exams in China, inviting international ophthalmologists to China for academic exchange and guidance, setting up scholarships for exceptional Chinese ophthalmologists to study in top international medical schools, and providing international charity eye care services to “Belt and Road” countries.

In 20 years, “Health Express” hospitals performed free surgeries for more than 192,000 poverty-stricken cataract patients, established 75 “Health Express” eye clinics and 40 DR centers, trained more than 20,000 grassroots ophthalmologists, screened about 76,000 diabetics and saved over 2,400 DR patients from loss of vision.

01 2015年，82岁的庞野老人在停靠于广西北海的“健康快车—澳门光明号”列车上做白内障摘除手术前的视力检查。老人曾参加过抗美援朝战争。

02 来自北京和广西北海的医生在“健康快车—澳门光明号”上做白内障摘除手术。

01 82-year-old Pang Ye, a Korean War veteran, going through a vision check before having a cataract removal procedure on board a “Health Express” train that was stopped in Guangxi’s Beihai Station. The photograph was taken in 2015.

02 Doctors from Beijing and Beihai performing a cataract removal procedure on board a train.

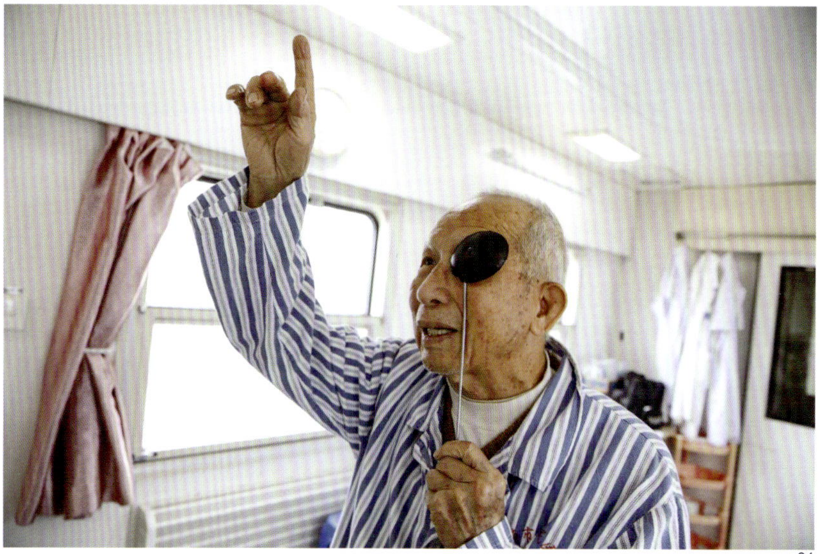

01

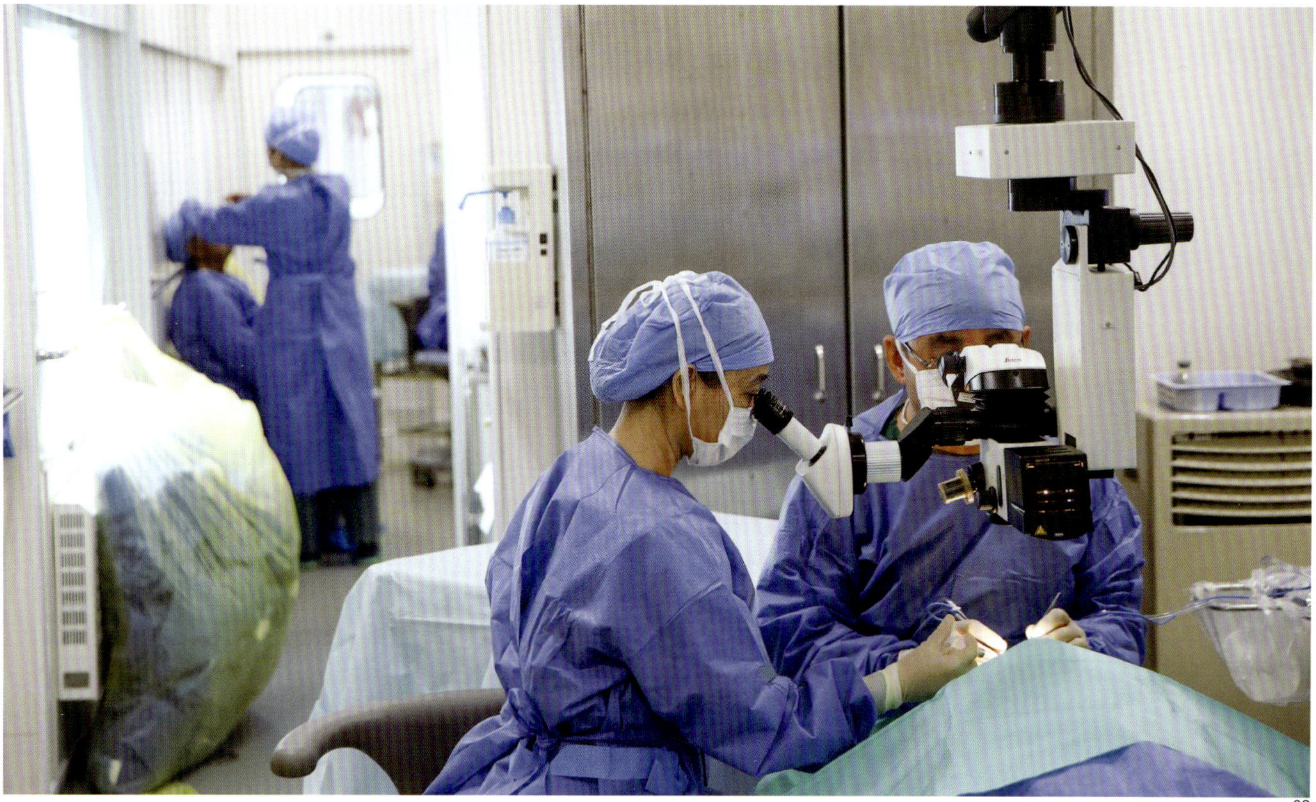

02

03

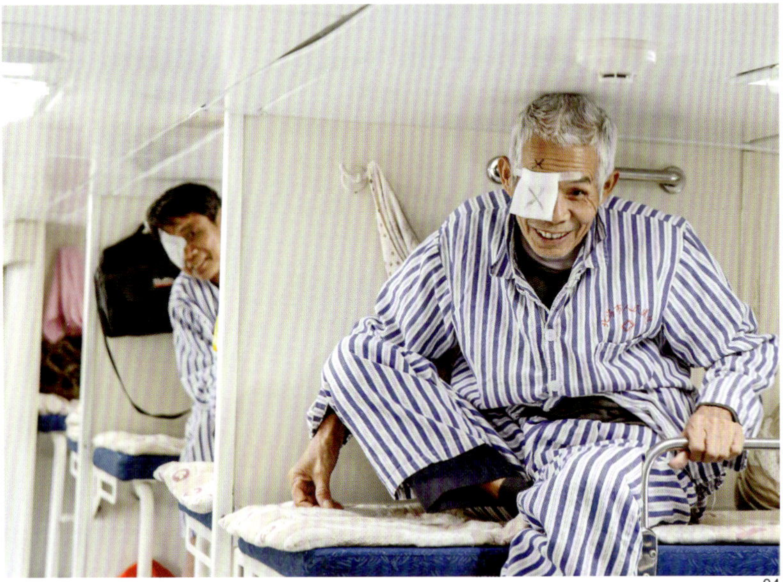

04

03 一名八旬患者在“健康快车—澳门光明号”上完成白内障摘除手术后，在护士搀扶下回到车厢休息观察。

04 一名完成白内障摘除手术的患者在列车上休息。

03 A patient in her 80s being helped to her bed for rest after surgery.

04 Rest after surgery.

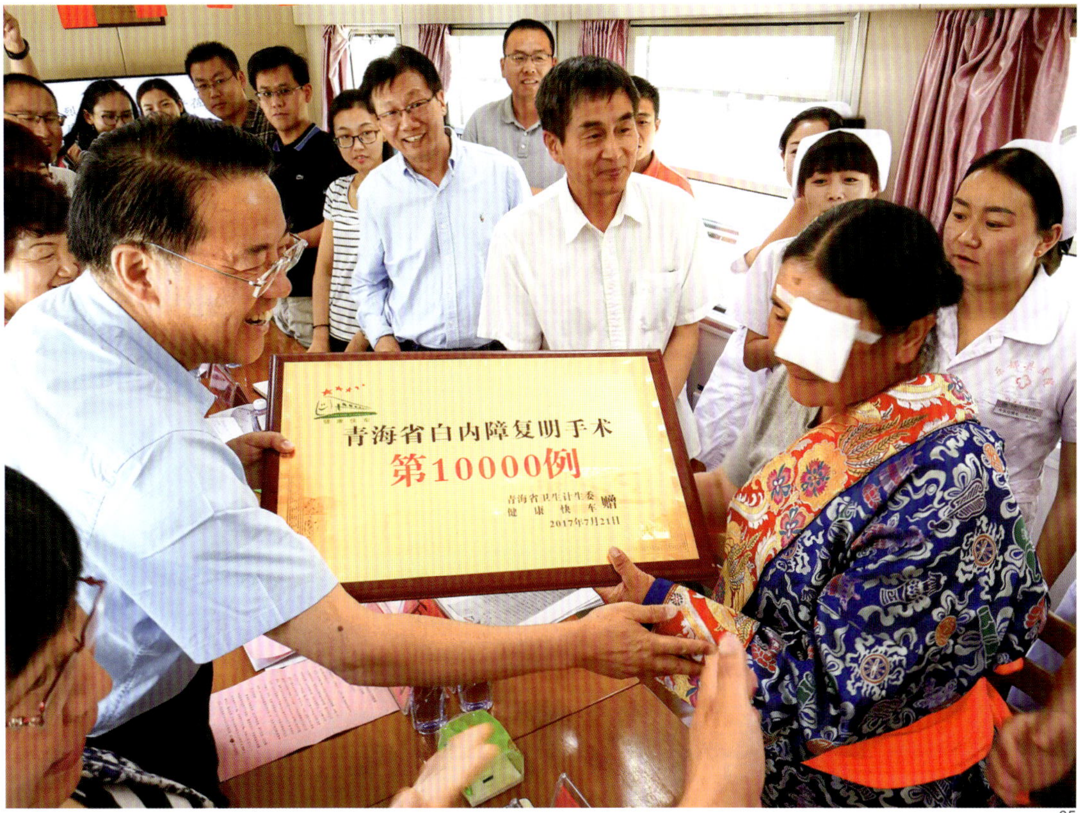

05

05 2017年7月21日，才太吉成为“健康快车”在青海省救治的第10000名贫困白内障患者。

05 July 21, 2017. Cai Taiji became the 10,000th cataract patient cured by “Health Express” in Qinghai Province.

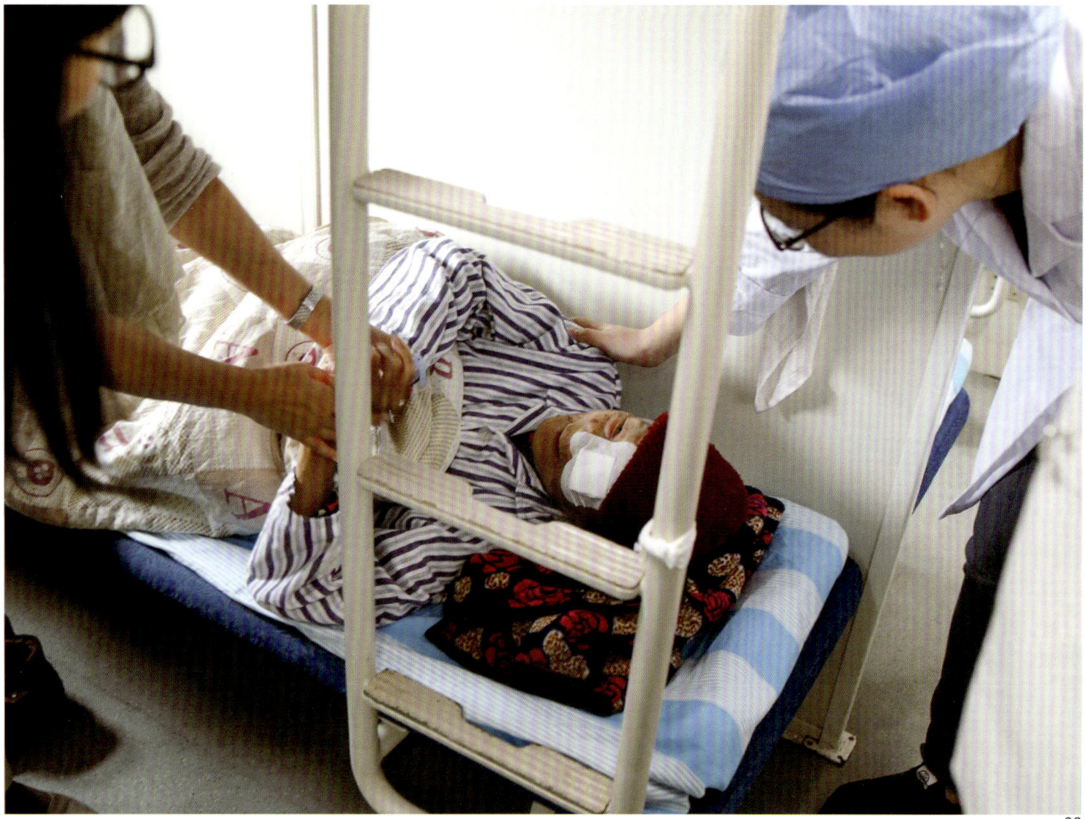

06

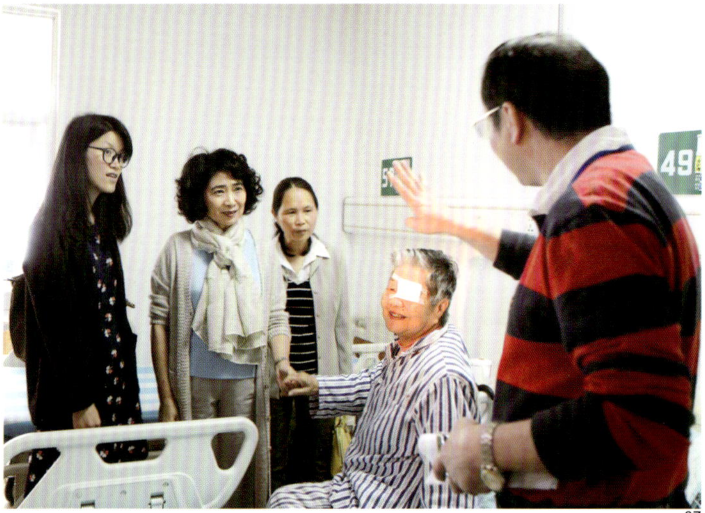

07

08

09

06 2017年11月9日，一名在“健康快车—澳门光明号”上接受手术的96岁白内障患者紧握工作人员的手表示感谢。
07 健康快车创会主席方黄吉雯女士（左二）与澳门基金会工作人员在医务人员的陪同下到贺州市人民医院健康快车眼科中心看望白内障患者。
08 一名在“健康快车—澳门光明号”上等待手术的白内障患者对医务人员竖起大拇指。
09 四列健康快车之一“澳门光明号”。

06 November 9, 2017. A 96-year-old cataract patient who has just been through a cataract removal procedure.
07 Nellie Fong Wong Kut-man (second left), founding president of Health Express, and the staff of the Macao Foundation, paying a visit to a cataract patient.
08 A cataract patient waiting for surgery gives a thumbs-up to medical workers.
09 “Macao Light,” one of the four “Health Express” hospitals.

敖汉旗“3+2”医疗救助新模式
Aohan Banner's Health Care Assistance Model

图/文　敖汉旗医保局
Photos and Text by Aohan Banner's Medical Insurance Bureau

内蒙古赤峰市敖汉旗是国家级贫困县。敖汉旗通过“产业引领、金融助推、合作互助、企业嫁接、收缩转移、资产收益、医疗救助、养老保障”八种模式推进脱贫工作，在医疗救助方面，创建了大病扶贫爱心基金，实施精准扶贫全民商业医疗补充保险，成效显著。

大病扶贫爱心基金是为解决贫困人口及其他贫困群体因病致贫返贫问题专门设立的一项大病救助基金。救助对象包括贫困人口、城乡低保人员、农村五保人员、城镇三无人员和重度残疾五类群体。大病就医费用先经城乡居民基本医疗保险和医保统筹内大病保险报销，再经民政、红十字会、残联、慈善总会等渠道合理救助，最后由大病扶贫爱心基金进行帮扶。2017年，敖汉旗又在爱心基金的基础上，按照“政府主导，社会参与，群众自筹，基金撬动”的原则，采取财政补一点儿、群众筹一点儿、大病爱心基金和民政等出一点儿的方式，为全民购买商业补充医疗保险，即精准扶贫全民商业医疗补充保险。

敖汉旗通过创新实施“基本医保及统筹内的大病保险、贫困人口政策倾斜、民政救助”加“商业补充保险、大病扶贫爱心基金”即“3+2”医

Aohan Banner, Chifeng City, Inner Mongolia is a national poverty-stricken county. The county promotes poverty alleviation via industrial development, financial support, cooperation and mutual assistance, business resources integration, farmers and herdsmen relocation, medical assistance, and pension guarantee. In terms of medical assistance, the county has established a Charity Fund for Relief of Poverty Caused by Serious Illnesses and has bought supplementary medical insurance for all of its targeted poor people.

The said Charity Fund was established to exclusively help relieve disease-induced poverty. Its beneficiaries include impoverished people, urban and rural residents living on minimum subsistence allowances, rural people qualified for the "Five Guarantee Program" (i.e. food, clothing, health care, housing and final expenses), urban people with no income, no ability to work and no support, and those with serious disability. Their medical expenses for serious illnesses will first be reimbursed through basic health insurance, serious illness insurance within the framework of the Social Medical Insurance Coordination Fund before being covered by reasonable support from the Civil Affairs Bureau, the Red Cross, the Disabled Persons' Federation, the China Charity Federation and other sources, and finally, by the Charity Fund. The Charity Fund is an umbrella policy that covers the remainder of the loss. In 2017, Aohan Banner bought for all of its targeted poor people commercial supplementary medical insurance, with money pooled from the government, the rank and file, the Charity Fund, the Civil Affairs Bureau and other sources.

疗救助新模式，使建档立卡贫困人口实际补偿比达到85%。

Through the health care assistance model, the documented poor received 85% of their health coverage in actual compensation.

01

02

01 大病扶贫结算服务平台为群众办理业务提供方便。结算服务平台是为包括扶贫人口在内的全旗人民结算医疗相关费用而建立的“一站式”服务平台。

02 民众在工作人员指导下使用敖汉旗医保局自助查询系统。

01 The one-stop medical expense settlement platform for all patients of the Banner.

02 Learning how to use a self-service health care information system.

03

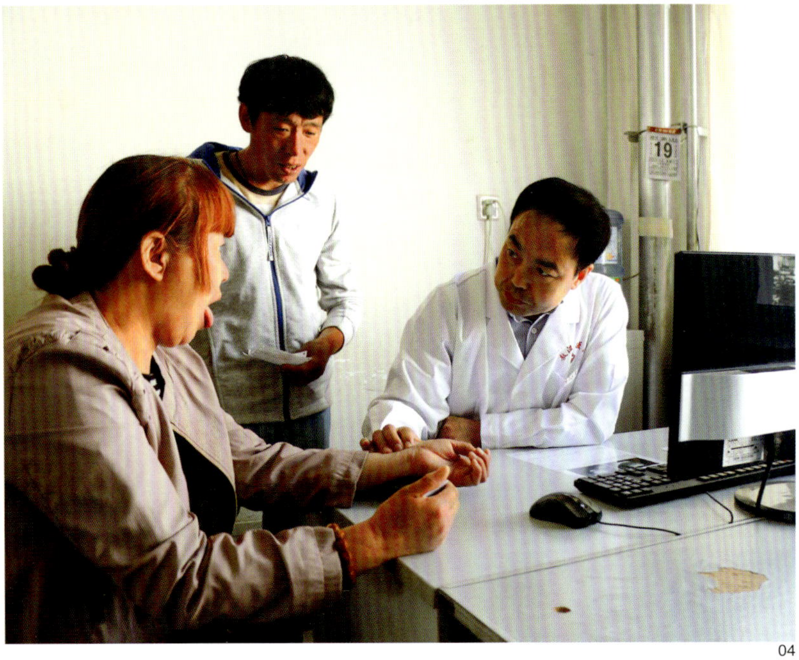

04

03 城乡居民集中缴纳参保费。
04 参保患者就近就医。
05 工作人员核实病人贫困情况。
06 患者家属在医保报销窗口前排队报销。

03 Paying insurance premium at counter.
04 Seeing a doctor close to home.
05 Poverty information verification.
06 Lining up for medical reimbursement.

05

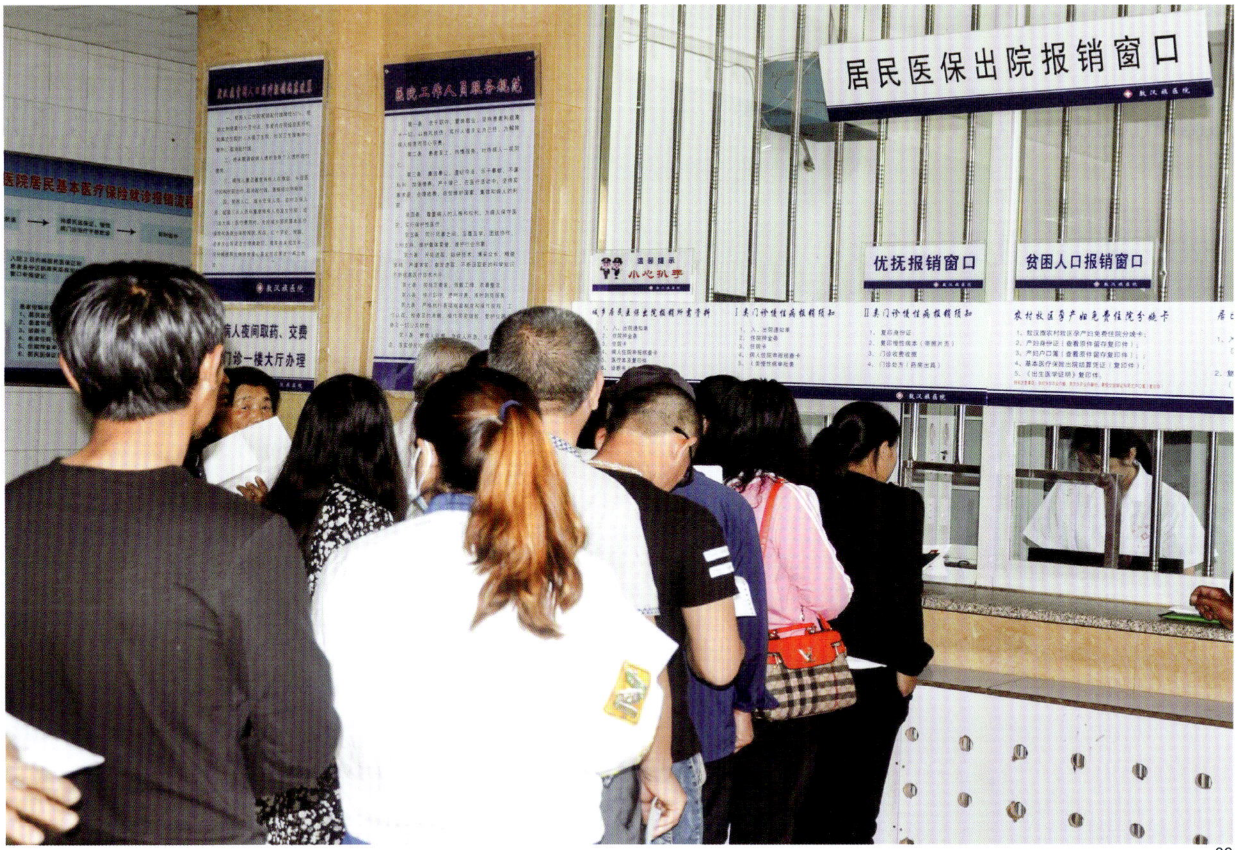

06

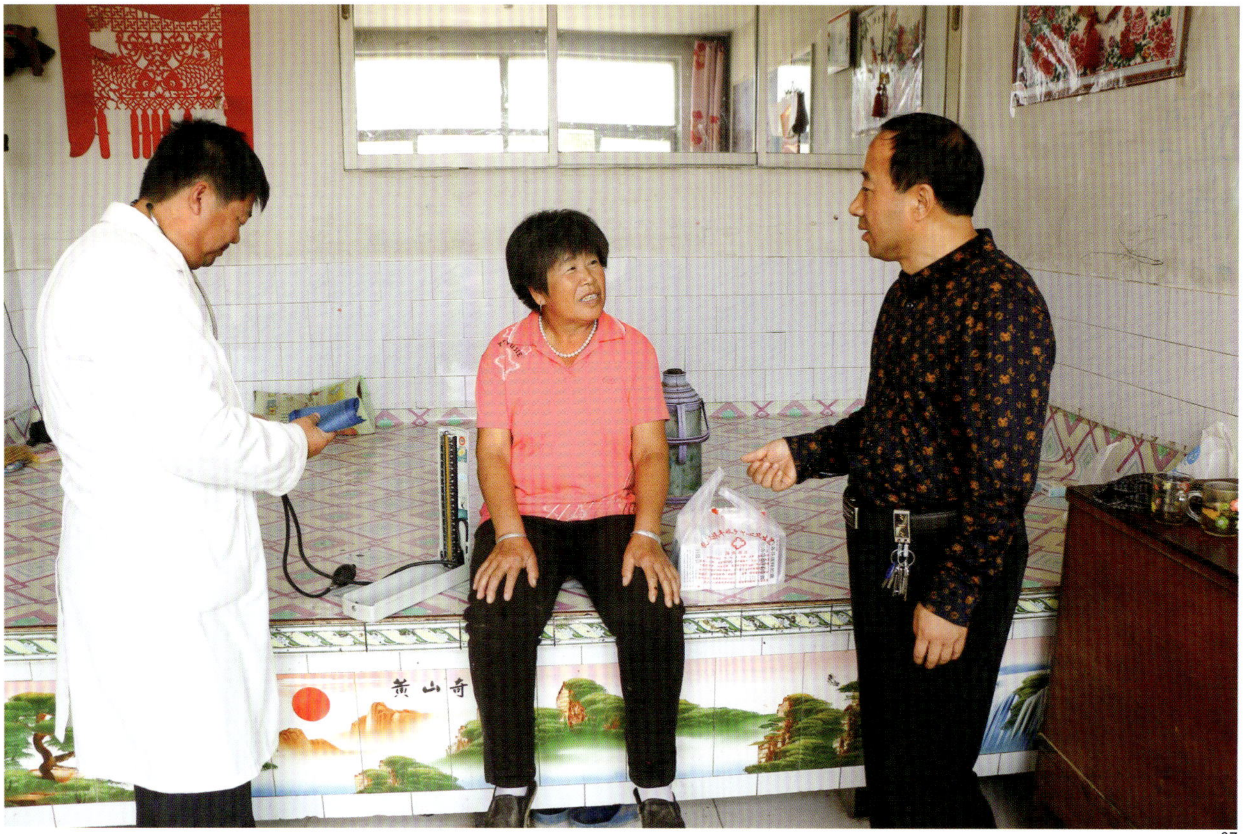

07

08

07 敖汉旗医保局工作人员对贫困患者进行回访并送药。

08 群众扫描二维码关注大病扶贫爱心基金。

07 Staff of the Healthcare Security Bureau of Aohan Banner paying a visit to an insured poor patient.

08 Scanning in the QR code of the Charity Fund.

09

09 爱心企业为敖汉旗大病扶贫爱心基金募捐。

09 Representatives of corporate donors to the Charity Fund.

处理好生态保护与扶贫开发的关系，加强贫困地区生态环境保护与治理修复，提升贫困地区可持续发展能力。逐步扩大对贫困地区和贫困人口的生态保护补偿，增设生态公益岗位，使贫困人口通过参与生态保护实现就业脱贫。

——《“十三五”脱贫攻坚规划》

We must balance eco-environmental protection on the one hand and poverty alleviation and development on the other. Specifically, eco-environment in poverty-stricken areas shall be protected, and sustainable development capacity be enhanced. We will gradually increase compensation for ecological protection in impoverished areas, create jobs in ecological public services, and help people out of poverty by involving them in eco-environmental protection.

——*National Plan for Poverty Alleviation During the 13th Five-Year Plan Period (2016-2020)*

绿水青山就是金山银山

生态保护扶贫

Alleviating Poverty by Protecting Eco-environment

塞罕坝，治沙止漠筑“绿色长城”
Saihanba, a “Green Great Wall” Against Desertification

图/文　魏晞（图03、09、12、13），张永新（图04、05、07），乔天富（图06、14、15），盛佳鹏（图08），艾广德（图10–11）
Photos and Text by Wei Xi (Photos 03, 09, 12, 13), Zhang Yongxin (Photos 04, 05 and 07), Qiao Tianfu (Photos 06, 14 and 15), Sheng Jiapeng (Photo 08) and Ai Guangde (Photos 10-11)

第三届联合国环境大会发布的2017年地球卫士奖，把“2017地球卫士·行动与激励奖”颁发给了塞罕坝林场。这是联合国最高环境荣誉奖项第一次颁发给河北。

50多年的坚守，塞罕坝林场三代人在昔日飞鸟不栖、黄沙遮天的荒原上，建设了112万亩世界上面积最大的人工林场，创造了沙地变绿洲、荒原变林海的“绿色奇迹”，以实际行动诠释了“绿水青山就是金山银山”的理念，铸就了牢记使命、艰苦创业、绿色发展的塞罕坝精神。

如今的塞罕坝生态效益显著，单位面积林木蓄积量是全国人工林平均水平的2.76倍，全国森林平均水平的1.58倍。塞罕坝每年为京津地区输送净水1.37亿立方米，释放氧气55万吨，成为守卫京津的重要生态屏障。塞罕坝机械林场集造林护林、森林旅游、苗木生产、林产品采集加工于一体，成为环境、社会、经济效益良好的绿色发展生态文明建设典范。

In 2017, the Saihanba Afforestation Community in Hebei Province won the honor of Champions of the Earth in the category of Inspiration and Action, the highest environmental honor provided by the United Nations.

For over 50 years, three generations of the Saihanba Forest Farm community have worked continuously to build the world's largest planted forest farm with an area of 1.12 million *mu* (around 74,667 hectares) and have done a “green miracle” turning a desert into an oasis and a wasteland into a sea of woods.

Today, Saihanba provides remarkable ecological benefits with a forest stock per unit area that is 2.76 times that of the average of all national planted forests and 1.58 times that of the average of all national forests, respectively. Every year, Saihanba purifies 137 million cubic meters of water and releases 550,000 tons of oxygen to the greater Beijing and Tianjin area, becoming an important ecological shield for this region. The current Saihanba Mechanical Forest Farm has become an integrated system of afforestation, forest protection, forest tourism, seedling production and forest product collection, and has become an exemplary case of green development that has brought about sound environmental, social and economic benefits.

01

02

01 1962年前后塞罕坝机械林场建场初期的照片（资料图）。

02 塞罕坝林场“一棵松”（资料图）。

03 这是塞罕坝一棵树龄近200年的“功勋树”，50多年前，正是在荒原上发现了这棵落叶松，确定了当地自然条件可种植大树，才建立了塞罕坝机械林场。

01 Saihanba Mechanical Forest Farm in 1962 (file photo).

02 The “Solitary” Larch Tree (file photo).

03 A larch tree about 200 years old. Discovery of this tree over 50 years ago led to the decision to build the Saihanba Mechanical Forest Farm here.

03

04

05

06

07

04 2011年8月13日，塞罕坝上的风力发电场。
05 2011年8月13日，晨雾笼罩的塞罕坝。
06 2017年9月11日，塞罕坝秋景如画。
07 2011年8月13日，塞罕塔风光。

04 A wind power plant in Saihanba, August 13, 2011.
05 Saihanba in morning mist, August 13, 2011.
06 Saihanba, September 11, 2017.
07 A pagoda in Saihanba, August 13, 2011.

08

08 2016年9月22日，河北承德木兰围场上奔跑的骏马。木兰围场又称清代皇家猎场，由塞罕坝国家森林公园、御道口草原森林风景区和红松洼国家自然保护区等三大景区组成。

09 塞罕坝林场已进入植树造林攻坚期。2011年以来，塞罕坝把土壤贫瘠和岩石裸露的石质阳坡作为绿化重点。在那些地带，有的土壤厚度只有几公分，有的坡度甚至达到46度，成功种植一棵树，需要花费更多的劳动和投入。

10 2017年7月12日，塞罕坝林场林木郁郁葱葱。

11 2017年7月12日，塞罕坝七星湖。

08 Galloping steeds on Mulan Paddock in Chengde, Hebei Province, September 22, 2016. Mulan Paddock, aka Qing Dynasty Royal Paddock, is made up of three major scenic spots, including Saihanba National Forest Park, Yudaokou Grassland and Forest Zone, and Hongsongwa National Nature Reserve.

09 Afforested rocky land. Planting trees on such land involves much more labor and other resources.

10 Saihanba Forest Farm, July 12, 2017.

11 Qixing Lake of Saihanba, July 12, 2017.

09

10

11

12

13

14

15

12 2017年7月11日，塞罕坝林场防火办副主任孙文国介绍林场防火情况，包括卫星监测、红外雷达探火系统、视频监控系统等。
13 “望海楼”是塞罕坝11座“夫妻望火楼”中的一座。在防火紧要期，夫妻防火员两人需要在山上连续坚守数月，每15分钟记录报送一次观测情况，夜晚也不间断。
14 2017年9月12日，间伐作业点储木场归楞作业。塞罕坝人秉持科学求实精神和“造林固本、经营培元”“三分造、七分管”的理念，尽心尽力“管好树”，实现了“越砍越好”的良性循环。
15 2017年9月11日，美术家为“全国劳动模范” 塞罕坝大唤起林场施工员许文江作画。

12 Sun Wenguo, deputy director of the Fire Prevention Office of the Saihanba Forest Farm, talks about fire prevention measures at the forest farm, including the satellite monitoring system, the infrared radar fire detection system, the video monitoring system, July 11, 2017.
13 Wanghai Tower, one of the 11 fire-watching towers at Saihanba. Fire watchers live in the mountain for months on end to watch out for fire and report their observations every 15 minutes, even at night.
14 Felling for better growth, September 12, 2017.
15 Xu Wenjiang, a model worker from Saihanba Dahuanqi Forest Farm, by his own portrait, September 11, 2017.

遏制生态退化　呵护三江源

Protecting Sanjiangyuan by Curbing Ecological Degradation

图/文　李全举（图01）、 赵凛松（图02）、 孙自法（图03）、胡贵龙（图04）、韩海丹（图05-06）、盛佳鹏（图07）、罗云鹏（图08）、孙燕初（图10）、张添福（图11）、孙睿（图12）
Photos and Text by Li Quanju (Photo 01), Zhao Linsong (Photo 02), Sun Zifa (Photo 03), Hu Guilong (Photo 04), Han Haidan (Photos 05-06), Sheng Jiapeng (Photo 07), Luo Yunpeng (Photo 08), Sun Yanchu (Photo 10), Zhang Tianfu (Photo 11) and Sun Rui (Photo 12)

中国最大的自然环境保护区——三江源自然保护区位于青藏高原腹地，因长江、黄河和澜沧江发源于此而得名，是中国乃至亚洲重要的生态屏障和水源涵养区。20世纪中期以来，受气候变化和人类活动等因素影响，三江源地区生态系统遭到严重的破坏。

2005年，国务院批准了《青海三江源自然保护区生态保护和建设总体规划》，一期工程于2005—2013年实施，总投资75亿元；二期工程于2014年初正式启动，取得了显著成效。

《三江源生态保护和建设二期工程规划中期省级自查评估报告》和年度监测报告显示，三江源地区生态系统退化趋势得到初步遏制，生态建设工程区生态环境明显好转，草原退化趋势明显减缓，森林生态功能逐渐增强，湿地生态系统面积扩大，荒漠化土地面积逐步减少，水源涵养功能明显提升，江河径流量逐渐增加，水土保持功能不断增强，生物多样性资源恢复加快，生态保护和建设成效凸显。此外，通过生态补偿、加强基础设施建设、支持当地发展生态畜牧业和旅游业等多种措施，农牧民生产生活方式发生重大变化，收入水平明显提高，2016年农牧民人均纯收入达到7300元，较2013年增长34.97%。

Sanjiangyuan National Nature Reserve (SNNR) in the heart of the Qinghai-Tibet Plateau is the largest nature reserve in China. Sanjiangyuan (literally origin of three rivers) is so called because the Yangtze, the Yellow and the Lancang River all originate from here. It is an important ecological shield and water conservation area in China and even all Asia. Since the mid-20th century, due to the influence of climate change and human activities, ecology of the Sanjiangyuan area has been seriously damaged.

In 2005, the State Council approved an Overall Plan to Protect and Develop the Sanjiangyuan Nature Reserve in Qinghai Province. The first phase of the project with a total investment of 7.5 billion yuan was carried out from 2005 to 2013, and the second phase initiated in early 2014 has seen significant progress.

A provincial mid-term assessment report and an annual monitoring report show that eco-environment in the project area has greatly improved as grassland degradation slowed down, wetland area grew, desertification went down, water and soil conservation got strengthened, and biodiversity resource recovery accelerated. Besides, through eco-compensation and strengthening of infrastructure building, support of local ecological animal husbandry and tourism and other measures, local farmers and herdsmen saw major change in their production and life style. In 2016, their per capita net income reached 7,300 yuan, a 34.97% increase over that of 2013.

01 2008年3月23日，2008青海高原热气球之旅——“世界水日”三江源热气球行动活动在青海三江源地区举行。

02 2013年10月18日，几只藏原羚在青藏公路边觅食，远处是青藏铁路。随着保护力度的加大，在青藏公路沿线的三江源保护区，野生动物种群数量恢复明显，以前很难看到的藏野驴、藏羚羊等动物在公路边随处可见。

01

02

01 World Water Day Hot-Air Balloon Travel in Sanjiangyuan, March 23, 2008.

02 Goats grazing by the Qinghai-Tibet Highway, October 18, 2013.

03

04

05

03 2014年4月12日，青海省果洛藏族自治州，州府所在地玛沁县雪后天晴。果洛平均海拔4200米以上，由于特殊的地理位置和自然环境，全境被列入三江源自然保护区内。

04 水草丰美的三江源区域。

05 曲麻莱县地处黄河正源和长江北源，位于三江源生态保护区腹地，素有“江河源头第一县”的美称。黄河发源于该县麻多乡约古宗列地区，长江北源主要源流均发源于县境内，是中国南北两大水系的主要水源涵养地。图为牧民在黄河源挂经幡祈福。

03 A sunny day after snow in Maqen, seat of government of Golog Tibetan Autonomous Prefecture, Qinghai Province. Average elevation of Golog is over 4,200 meters. Because of its unique geographical location and natural environment, the entire prefecture is encompassed in the Sanjiangyuan Nature Reserve.

04 The Sanjiangyuan area with abundant water and grass.

05 Herdsmen in Qumarleb County praying for good luck by hanging prayer flags at the headwaters of the Yellow River.

06

06 曲麻莱县僧人举行祭河民俗。
07 在曲麻莱县境内远眺玉珠峰。

06 Monks in Qumarleb County offering a sacrifice to the river.
07 A remote view of Yuzhu Peak from Qumarleb County.

07

08 2016年8月26日，在三江源国家公园长江源（可可西里）园区治多管理处索加乡君曲村，生态管护员骑马巡护。三江源国家公园是中国首个国家公园，园区总面积12.31万平方公里。这里管护面积大、路程远且交通不便，组织马队便于开展日常巡护。

09 三江源国家公园黄河源园区纪念碑（资料图）。

08

09

08 Park rangers patrolling on horses at Junqu Village, Sokya Township, Zhidoi County at the origin of the Yangtze River in the Sanjiangyuan National Park (in Hoh Xil), August 26, 2016. Sanjiangyuan National Park, the first national park in China, has a total area of 123,100 square kilometers.

09 Monument marking the origin of the Yellow River in Sanjiangyuan National Park (file photo).

10

11

12

10 2017年5月，聚集在三江源保护区的怀孕母藏羚羊在可可西里国家级保护区管理局工作人员以及环保志愿者的保护下，通过青藏公路，向可可西里腹地卓乃湖迁徙产仔。

11 2017年12月16日，三江源国有自然资源资产管理局在青海西宁正式挂牌，标志着三江源国有自然资源资产管理体制试点全面启动。

12 2018年，青海三江源水源入选“中国好水”。图为地处三江源自然保护区腹地的年宝玉则（又称“果洛山”）。

10 In May 2017, pregnant Tibetan antelopes in the Sanjiangyuan Reserve crossing the Qinghai-Tibet Highway to migrate to Zonag Lake in the heart of Hoh Xil to give birth, under the escort of staff of the Hoh Xil National Nature Reserve and environmental protection volunteers.

11 On December 16, 2017, the State-Owned Natural Resources and Assets Administration of Sanjiangyuan was officially established in Xining, Qinghai, marking the inauguration of the pilot management system of state-owned natural resources and assets in Sanjiangyuan.

12 Water at Sanjiangyuan was rated as “China’s Quality Water” in 2018. The photo shows Mt. Nyanpo Yutse (aka Mt. Golog) in the heart of the Nature Reserve.

“天保工程”20年　花城换新颜

“NFP Project” Gives Panzhihua City a New Look in Two Decades

图/文　章轲（图01-04）、刘忠俊（图05-07）、刘龙（图08）
Photos and Text by Zhang Ke (Photos 01-04), Liu Zhongjun (Photos 05-07) and Liu Long (Photo 08)

攀枝花，一座以花命名的国家森林城市，是国家“天保工程”的发源地。

20世纪60年代，因建设需要，攀枝花及上游地区大量木材被采伐并运到全国各地，攀枝花累计贡献了600万立方米木材，水土流失严重，金沙江两岸荒山触目惊心。

1998年8月23日，四川省委、省政府下发《四川省人民政府关于实施天然林资源保护工程的决定》（简称“天保工程”），攀枝花市、甘孜州、阿坝州、凉山州、乐山市、雅安市在全国率先实施天然林保护工程。从此，攀枝花打响了声势浩大的天然林资源保卫战，全力开展天然林资源保护、退耕还林和野生动植物保护及自然保护区建设工程。经过不懈努力，这里的生态环境发生了巨大变化，取得了可观的效益。

至2017年，攀枝花拥有林业用地831.2万亩，其中林地635.8万亩，森林覆盖率60.1%，森林活立木蓄积4066万立方米。1998年，全市林业总产值为6654万元，而20年后增长了54倍。攀枝花逐渐构建起较为发达的林业产业发展体系，预计至2025年，林业总产值在2015年基础上翻一番，达到60亿元，使林业产业逐步发展成为农村经济的重要支柱产业，让更多农民享受绿色经济效益。2014年，四川省在

Panzhihua, a national forest city named after a flower (bombax flower), is the origin of China's "Natural Forest Protection (NFP) Project."

In the 1960s, in order to meet the needs of national construction, numerous trees in Panzhihua and other places on the upper reaches of the Yangtze River were felled and delivered to all parts of China. Panzhihua had contributed a total of six million cubic meters of timber, resulting in serious erosion and shocking barrenness on the two banks of the Jinsha River, another name of the Yangtze.

On August 23, 1998, the CPC Sichuan Provincial Committee and Sichuan Provincial Government issued a Decision to Launch the Natural Forest Protection Project (NFP Project), marking the start of the national project in Panzhihua City, Aba Prefecture, Liangshan Prefecture, Leshan City and Ya'an City. After relentless effort, Panzhihua substantially improved its eco-environment and achieved remarkable social and economic benefits.

In 2017, Panzhihua's forestry land amounted to 8.321 million *mu* (around 554,133 hectares), including 6.358 million *mu* (around 423,867 hectares) of forest cover, or 60.1% of the city's total land area, and 40.66 million cubic meters of standing forests. Total forestry output value of the city saw a 54-fold surge over that of 1998 to reach 66.54 million yuan. It is expected that by 2025, total forestry output value would double that of 2015 to reach 6 billion yuan, so that forestry-related industries would gradually become important pillar industries for rural economy and more farmers would enjoy the benefits of the "green economy."

In 2014, Sichuan Province pioneered the concept of "forest-based health services" and Panzhihua City began to develop forest-based health industry. By 2016, this city earned a total

全国率先提出推进“森林康养”理念，攀枝花市以此为契机，大力发展森林康养产业。2016年，全市实现生态旅游和森林康养收入13亿元。

income of 1.3 billion yuan from eco-tourism and forest-based health industry.

01 攀枝花市是我国天然林资源保护工程的发源地。
02 2017年10月16日，攀枝花市城市风光。
03 2017年10月17日，攀枝花市米易县城市风光。

01 Panzhihua City is the origin of the “Natural Forest Protection Project” in China.
02 Panzhihua City, October 16, 2017.
03 A view of Miyi County, Panzhihua City, October 17, 2017.

01

02

03

04

04 2017年10月17日，米易县普威林业局护林员赵小波带着工具上山。

05 2017年2月15日，攀枝花市东区银江镇阿署达新村一角。利用优质的阳光、空气资源，这里已从过去的贫困村变成了闻名遐迩的国际康养“城”。

04 Zhao Xiaobo, a ranger of the Puwei Forestry Bureau in Miyi County comes to work, October 17, 2017.

05 Ashuda New Village in Yinjiang Town, Panzhihua City, February 15, 2017.

05

06

07

08

06 2017年2月15日，俯瞰阿署达新村全景。
07 2017年2月15日，阳光下，阿署达新村的三角梅。
08 攀枝花市的攀枝花树和蓝天。

06 A bird's eye view of Ashuda New Village, February 15, 2017.
07 Bougainvillea spectabilis blossoming in the sunlight. Ashuda New Village, February 15, 2017.
08 A bombax tree under the blue sky, Panzhihua City.

水土滋养重现开都河流域之美
Restoration of the Beauty of Kaidu River Basin

图/文　确·胡热（图01–06、08）、张正友（图07）、汤桂珍（图09）
Photos and Text by Que Hure (Photos 01-06, 08), Zhang Zhengyou (Photo 07) and Tang Guizhen (Photo 09)

开都河发源于天山的哈尔特山口，流域内有全国最大的内陆淡水湖博斯腾湖和中国第二大草原巴音布鲁克草原。开都河是巴音郭楞蒙古自治州的母亲河及农业灌溉的重要水源。在西部开发和产业发展过程中，部分行业忽视了长远生态效益，致使开都河流域出现较为严重的水土流失和生态失调。

为保护开都河流域生态环境，新疆维吾尔自治区出台了“开都河流域水土保持生态建设规划”，并制定了一系列措施，如在平原地区修建农田防护林网以提高农田覆盖度，减少冲积平原区的土壤风蚀；在山谷出口修建谷坊、塘坝等工程设施，减少水蚀和泥土下泄；在重要水源涵养地采取保护措施，减少人为扰动和牲畜啃食等。

巴州博湖县把湿地保护作为生态文明建设的重要内容，以“生态引领、绿色发展、全域旅游、幸福宜居”为发展目标，推进博斯腾湖流域生态环境综合治理，实施开都河三角洲水源地建设、环博斯腾湖湿地生物治碱工程、博斯腾湖国家湿地公园湿地保护与恢复、博斯腾湖生态环境保护试点项目、人工育苇等一大批生态修复工程。湿地生态功能和水体修复得到明显改善，环湖湿地面积逐年扩大，水生生物不断多样。2017年底，新疆博斯腾湖国家湿地公园通过国家试点建设验收，正式成为“国家湿地公园”，这对促进湿地

The Kaidu River originates from the Hargat Valley in Tianshan. Within the Kaidu River Basin are Lake Bosten, the largest inland freshwater lake in China, and Bayanbulak Grassland, the second largest grassland in China. The Kaidu River is the mother river of the Bayingolin Mongolian Autonomous Prefecture and an important source of water for agricultural irrigation. During the process of western development, due to neglect of long-term ecological interests in some sectors, the Kaidu River Basin became a victim of serious water and soil erosion and ecological imbalance.

To protect the eco-environment in the Kaidu River Basin, Xinjiang Uygur Autonomous Region has introduced a Plan for Water and Soil Conservation and Ecological Development in the Kaidu River Basin, and took a series of measures, including: 1) build farmland shelterbelt networks in flat areas to increase farmland coverage and reduce soil erosion in alluvial plains caused by wind; 2) build check dams, small reservoirs and other facilities near the valley entrances to reduce water erosion and mud drainage; 3) protect key water conservation areas and reduce human interference and animal grazing.

Bohu County in Bayingolin Prefecture prioritized wetland protection as an important part of its ecological development drive. To improve the overall eco-environment in the Bosten River Basin, the county launched multiple ecological recovery projects, including the Kaidu River Delta Water Source Construction Project, the Biological Alkali Control Project, the Bosten Lake Wetland Project, the Bosten Lake Eco-environmental Protection Pilot Project and the Reed Planting Project. As a result, the ecological functions of the wetland and water resources restoration saw significant improvement. Wetland area around the lake expanded year by year and aquatic species kept growing. By the end of 2017, the Bosten Lake, as a pilot project, was formally designated as a national wetland park. This further protected the wetland's eco-environment, enhanced the image and reputation of Bohu as an ecological

生态环境保护、提升"生态博湖"形象和知名度、拉动当地旅游及经济社会发展等方面起到积极促进作用，旅游扶贫的重要作用也得到更充分显现。

county, stimulated local tourism and socio-economic development, and further highlighted the importance of tourism in relieving poverty.

01

02

01 2017年8月17日，在新疆生产建设兵团第二师21团段航拍的开都河。
02 2017年8月18日，在新疆焉耆回族自治县段航拍的开都河。

01 Aerial view of the Kaidu River in the jurisdiction of the 21st Regiment of 2nd Division of the Xinjiang Production and Construction Corps, August 17, 2017.
02 Aerial view of the Kaidu River in the jurisdiction of Yanqi Hui Autonomous County, Xinjiang, August 18, 2017.

03

04

05

03 2017年8月18日在新疆博湖县段航拍开都河水流入博斯腾湖。

04 2017年10月11日航拍博斯腾湖湿地。

05 2016年9月13日，博斯腾湖莲花湖景区。

03 Where the Kaidu River joins the Bosten Lake in the jurisdiction of Bohu County, Xinjiang, August 18, 2017.

04 Aerial view of the Bosten Lake Wetland, October 11, 2017.

05 Lianhua Lake Scenic Area of the Bosten Lake Park, September 13, 2016.

06

07

06 2016年初冬，博斯腾湖湖畔芦苇泛黄，碧水蓝天，水鸟成群。

07 2015年6月26日，第二届中国博斯腾湖国际帆船公开赛在新疆博湖县大河口（西海渔村）景区举行，来自国内外的代表队在博斯腾湖畔扬帆竞速。

06 Bosten Lake in early winter, 2016.

07 Contestants racing near the shore of Lake Bosten on June 26, 2015, during an International Sailing Open held in the Dahekou Scenic Area (Xihai Fishing Village) in Bohu County, Xinjiang.

08

09

08 2016年12月17日，天鹅在新疆和静县巴音布鲁克湿地嬉戏。
09 2016年5月23日，夕阳下的巴音布鲁克湿地。

08 The swans of Bayanbulak Wetland in Hejing County, Xinjiang, December 17, 2016.
09 The Bayanbulak Wetland under the setting sun, May 23, 2016.

统筹社会救助体系，促进扶贫开发与社会保障有效衔接，完善农村低保、特困人员救助供养等社会救助制度，健全农村“三留守”人员和残疾人关爱服务体系，实现社会保障兜底。

——《“十三五”脱贫攻坚规划》

We must coordinate social welfare systems and promote the effective integration of poverty relief development and social security. We must improve the social welfare systems such as subsistence allowances for rural poor and for the extremely poor, improve the system of care and service for the left-behind children, women and old people and the disabled in rural areas, so that everyone in society will be entitled to social security.

——*National Plan for Poverty Alleviation During the 13th Five-Year Plan Period (2016-2020)*

情暖底层　大爱无疆

兜底保障

Guaranteed Social Security for Those at the Bottom Rung of Society

光明驿站　情暖留守儿童
Sunshine Service Center Cares for Left-behind Children

图/文　马勇（图01、03），李昌兵（图02），郑贤列（图04），宋卫星（图05），牛路（图06），刘勤利（图07-10），吕贞（图11）
Photos and Text by Ma Yong (Photos 01-03), Li Changbing (Photo 02), Zheng Xianlie (Photo 04), Song Weixing (Photo 05), Niu Lu (Photo 06), Liu Qinli (Photos 07-10) and Lü Zhen (Photo 11)

2017年8月12日，安徽省第101家“光明驿站”在铜陵市西联镇漫园成立。“光明驿站”将通过实施“光明基金”爱心助学、激励帮扶、圆梦计划等方式，为留守儿童、贫困大学生撑起一片爱的天空。

“光明驿站”是国网安徽省电力公司自2012年开始，整合志愿活动资源，在全省范围内统筹实施的以关爱留守儿童为主题的志愿服务项目。在给留守儿童送上物质关爱的同时，其通过“爱心妈妈”“知心姐姐”结对帮扶，化解留守儿童心灵上的“亲情饥渴”，呵护他们健康成长。“光明驿站”荣获了“2012年度全国优秀志愿服务项目”二等奖。

作为农村劳务输出大省，安徽省有360多万留守儿童，该省将建设农村留守流动儿童活动室作为政府民生工程。

On August 12, 2017, the 101st “Sunshine Service Center” in Anhui Province was set up in Manyuan, Xilian Town, Tongling City. Sunshine Service Center aims at providing philanthropic assistance to the left-behind school children and impoverished college students via Sunshine Fund and help realize their dreams.

Sunshine Service Center is a voluntary service project initiated by the State Grid Anhui Electric Power Co., Ltd. in 2012 after integrating volunteer resources of Anhui Province. Its mission is to care for left-behind children by providing them both material and spiritual assistance. The project also quenches their thirst for family love by assigning them nominal moms or sisters so that they may grow up healthy. Sunshine Service Center won second prize from the “National Outstanding Volunteer Service Project for 2012.”

As a major source of migrant workers in China, Anhui has over 3.6 million left-behind children. The province will build activity centers for left-behind children in rural areas as part of the provincial government’s bid to promote people’s livelihood.

01

02

01 2012年6月1日，安徽省首个留守儿童"光明驿站"在宿州市桃园镇邱寨希望小学挂牌。

02 2013年1月18日，和县功桥镇考塘小学"光明驿站活动室"揭牌，志愿者教小朋友学习电脑知识。

01 Grand opening of Anhui's first Sunshine Service Center at the Hope Elementary School in Qiuzhai Village, Taoyuan Town, Suzhou City, June 1, 2012.

02 Volunteers teaching children how to use computers at Kaotang Elementary School in Gongqiao Town, Hexian County, January 18, 2013.

03

04

05

03 2014年1月17日，“爱心妈妈”给宿州市桃园镇邱寨希望小学留守儿童送来保暖用品。

04 2015年2月3日，安徽省第80座“光明驿站”在六安市金寨县汤家汇镇金刚台村梅河小学挂牌成立。孩子们在“光明驿站”里下棋。

05 2015年5月29日，滁州市全椒县西王乡隆兴村小学“光明驿站”揭牌，该校学生收到了捐赠的万余册课外图书及百余件文体学习用品。

03 A nominal mom sending winter clothing to a left-behind kid at Hope Elementary School in Qiuzhai Village, Taoyuan Town, Suzhou City, January 17, 2014.

04 On February 3, 2015, the 80th Sunshine Service Center opened at Meihe Elementary School in Jingangtai Village, Tangjiahui Town, Jinzhai County, Lu'an City. The children are playing a traditional Chinese game at the center.

05 On May 29, 2015, a Sunshine Service Center opened in Longxing Village Elementary School in Xiwang Township, Quanjiao County, Chuzhou City. The school received over 10,000 donated extracurricular books and over a hundred stationery and sporting goods.

06

06 2015年12月2日，蚌埠市蓝马甲志愿服务队在蚌埠市长青乡小学“光明驿站”举行“结对帮扶送温暖”活动。

07 2016年5月30日，志愿者在亳州市五马镇八里小学“光明驿站”里与留守儿童一起迎接儿童节。

07

06 December 2, 2015. The Blue Jacket Volunteers' Team of Bengbu City hosting an event through which each volunteer would pair up with a student who needs help at the city's Changqing Township Elementary School.

07 Volunteers and left-behind children celebrating Children's Day at the Sunshine Service Center in Bali Elementary School, Wuma Town, Bozhou City, May 30, 2016.

08

09

10

08 2016年5月30日，志愿者与亳州市五马镇八里小学留守儿童共迎“六一”，通过踩气球游戏锻炼孩子们的反应能力。

09 2016年5月30日，志愿者与亳州市五马镇八里小学留守儿童共迎“六一”，通过套圈游戏教育孩子们用付出获取收获。

10 2016年5月30日，志愿者与亳州市五马镇八里小学留守儿童一起跳绳，锻炼孩子们的协助能力。

08 Volunteers and left-behind children playing games, May 30, 2016, two days before Children's Day.

09 A game with rewards, May 30, 2016.

10 Rope skipping, May 30, 2016.

11

11 2017年8月12日，第101家“光明驿站”在安徽铜陵西联镇漫园成立，青年志愿者同受资助的孩子合影。

11 Volunteers and aided children at Manyuan, Xilian Town, Tongling City, Anhui Province, August 12, 2017. The 101st Sunshine Service Center of Anhui Province was set up that day.

老有所依　养老服务新模式

A New Model of Senior Care Service

图/文　董乃德
Photos and Text by Dong Naide

山东省邹平县魏桥镇老人入住阳光佳苑养老服务中心后，在衣食起居上得到了良好的照顾，工作人员还定期给老人们提供医疗保健服务，提供多种适宜的休闲娱乐方式，让老人们安享晚年好时光。

魏桥镇养老服务中心于2015年10月投入使用，是山东省首家乡镇级“公建民营”养老机构，由魏桥镇政府投资建设，引进青岛阳光佳苑养老服务管理有限公司负责项目运营管理，形成“政府统一管理、专业团队运营、职权明晰、优势互补”的养老服务新模式，为当地五保户、失能、失智老人提供专业规范化养老服务。该中心分为ABCD四个区，A区为综合服务楼，B区为社会养老区，C、D两区则是五保老人居住区。

作为山东省确定的养老服务业综合改革试点县，邹平县在完善养老服务体系的过程中，鼓励和吸引社会民间资本参与养老服务，形成企业或个人完全投资、村集体投入以及公建民营等多种方式相为协调互为补充的投资形式。同时，为居家养老服务的社区配送、家政、医疗等十余家企业应运而出，为有需求的老年人，特别是高龄、空巢、独居、失能、失智、生活贫困的老年人，提供托养、助医、健康、休闲、集中就餐和上门照护等服务，适合老年人文化娱乐、精神慰藉服务也更加多样化。

After moving into Sunshine Jiayuan Senior Care Service Center, seniors of Weiqiao Town, Zouping County, Shandong Province had their activities of daily living taken good care of. The center also provides seniors regular health care and suitable leisure and recreational activities, so that they may fully enjoy their later years.

The Senior Care Service Center of Weiqiao Town opened for business in October 2015. It provides standard and specialized service to local seniors who have no source of income, no ability to take care of themselves or are otherwise handicapped. The center is divided into four sections: the service building complex (Section A), the community senior care unit (Section B) and seniors entitled to guaranteed benefits of food, clothing, medical care, housing and final expenses (Sections C and D).

As a pilot county for comprehensive senior care reform in Shandong, Zouping County absorbs social capital so that investment in senior care services may come from enterprises, individuals and village collectives. More than a dozen enterprises specializing in services such as community delivery, housekeeping and medical care have emerged to serve seniors in need, especially those who are older, empty nested, living alone or in poverty, and physically or mentally handicapped. Typical services provided can include nursing, medical care assistance, recreation, collective dinning and in-home care. Meanwhile, entertainment and spiritual consolation services suitable for seniors have become diversified.

01 邹平县魏桥镇养老服务中心的工作人员精心照料老人。

01 A staff member at the Senior Care Center in Weiqiao Town, Zouping County, Shandong Province is taking good care of an old lady.

01

02

02 魏桥镇养老服务中心的工作人员指导老人进行肢体保健锻炼。

02 Teaching the elderly to do a fitness exercise.

03 魏桥镇养老服务中心的工作人员在为老人喂饭。

03 A nurse feeding a senior lady.

03

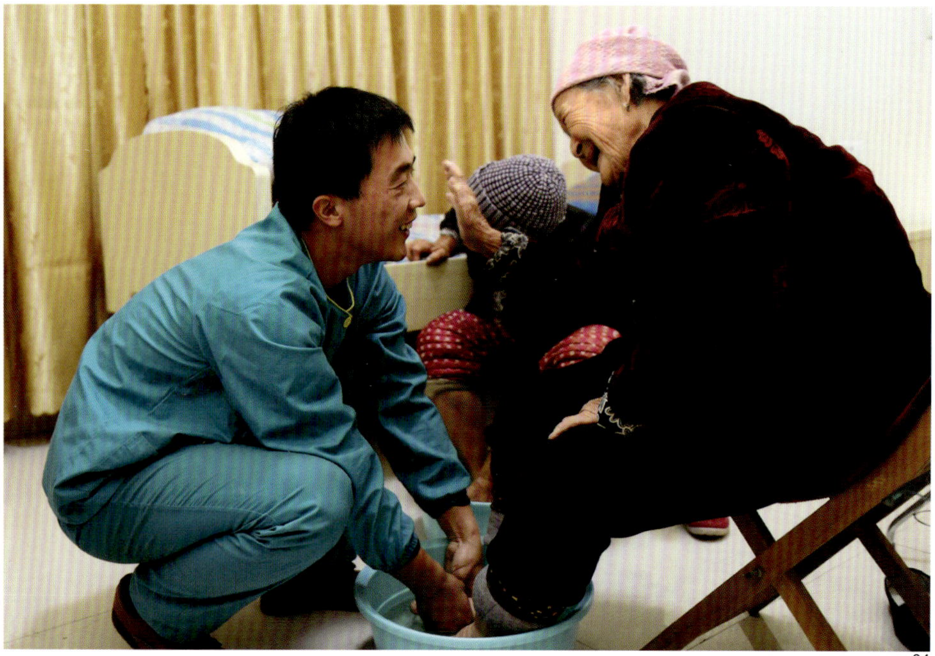

04

04 魏桥镇养老服务中心的工作人员晚饭后例行为老人洗脚。
05 魏桥镇养老服务中心的工作人员推着老人散步。

04 Washing a senior's feet.
05 A nurse and a senior at Weiqiao Senior Care Center.

05

06 焦桥镇牛家社区老年公寓的工作人员为刚入住的老人准备新被褥。该老年公寓将吸收周边村庄的老人入住。
07 焦桥镇牛家社区老年公寓阅览室。

06 Preparing beddings for a new recruit at a community senior care center.
07 Reading room in a seniors' apartment in Jiaoqiao Town.

06

07

08

08 焦桥镇牛家社区老年公寓的老人在下象棋。
09 焦桥镇牛家社区老年公寓的老人一起整理花卉，其乐融融。

08 A game of chess at a seniors' apartment.
09 Flower fans.

09

10

11

10 韩店镇西王村幸福院内的老人在唱歌娱乐。
11 志愿者来为台子镇老年福利服务中心的老人表演节目，老人们乐开怀。

10 Musical performance by seniors of Xiwang Village, Handian Town.
11 Enjoying musical performance by volunteers.

12

13

12 邹平爱心联盟的工作人员和台子镇老年福利服务中心的老人一起包水饺。
13 台子镇老年福利服务中心的工作人员为老人送饭。

12 Making dumplings together.
13 Staff members of a senior care center in Taizi Town are serving food to an elderly.

爱心超市
Philanthropic Supermarket

图/文　何五昌
Photos and Text by He Wuchang

近年，“爱心超市”这种由政府指导推动、社会各界广泛参与的扶贫济困模式，在全国多地出现。爱心超市有效地把社会各界慈善资源整合到平台上来，为当地低保家庭、大病重病家庭、孤寡老人儿童等困难群众提供免费、廉价的日常生活用品，提供就业机会，同时也为具有爱心的个人、机构提供捐赠爱心的场所。

观音堂林站位于河南省宝丰县西部山区，这里常年缺水，耕地面积较少，建档立卡贫困户较为集中，其中余家村条件更为恶劣。当地政府对余家村贫困户实施了异地搬迁，并建立了万青农业扶贫基地和“爱心超市”等扶贫项目。2018年1月19日，位于观音堂林站异地扶贫搬迁点余家花苑新村的“爱心超市”开业，贫困群众可用鸡蛋、花椒、蜂蜜等物品在超市兑换等价的米、面、油、衣、被等基本生活必需品，也可以购买到低于市场价5%～10%的商品，部分困难群众还可以在超市打工，缓解生活困难。

In recent years, Philanthropic Supermarket, a platform for poverty alleviation guided and promoted by the government and involving participation of all circles of society, have emerged in many parts of China. Philanthropic Supermarkets effectively integrate charity resources of all social circles to provide free or affordable items of daily necessities and work opportunities for local families receiving subsistence allowances or afflicted with serious illnesses and for the widowed, the elderly and orphans. Meanwhile it provides a venue where philanthropic individuals and organizations can make donations to impoverished families and individuals.

The Guanyintang Forestry Station located in the western mountain area of Baofeng County, Henan Province is an arid place of small farmland acreage and with many documented poor households. Yujia Village in this county is especially worse off. The county government therefore relocated the poor households of Yujia Village so that they may benefit from the newly established Wanqing Agricultural Poverty Alleviation Base and Philanthropic Supermarkets. On January 19, 2018, a Philanthropic Supermarket in Yujia Huayuan New Village, a relocation site located at the Guanyintang Forestry Station, opened for business. At the supermarket, low-income people can trade eggs, pepper and honey for daily necessities of equivalent value such as rice, flour, oil, clothing and bedding, or they can buy merchandise at prices 5-10% below market price. Some impoverished people can also choose to work at the supermarket to help make a living.

01 观音堂林站异地扶贫搬迁点余家花苑新村“爱心超市”开业。

01 Opening of a Philanthropic Supermarket in Yujia Huayuan New Village, a relocation site at Guanyintang Forestry Station.

01

02

02 “爱心超市”提供放心肉供村民选购。

02 A villager buying meat at the Philanthropic Supermarket in Yujia Huayuan New Village.

03 村民在“爱心超市”选购生活用品。

03 Shopping for items of daily necessity at the Philanthropic Supermarket.

03

04

05

06

04 崔家村村民张云提着鸡蛋到“爱心超市”兑换生活用品。张云家人因车祸失去劳动力，导致贫困。在当地畜牧局的帮扶下，她开始养鸡养猪，争取早日脱贫。

05 “爱心超市”的工作人员在清点张云（右）带来的鸡蛋。

06 “爱心超市”的员工张红丽在整理蔬菜。她家因病致贫，在这里打工每个月可收入1000多元。

04 Zhang Yun, a woman from the Cuijia Village, trades eggs for other items at the Philanthropic Supermarket. Due to a car accident, Zhang Yun's husband lost his ability to work and her family became poor. With help from the local animal husbandry bureau, Zhang started a career raising chickens and pigs in hopes of getting richer.

05 A shop assistant counting the eggs brought by Zhang Yun (right).

06 Zhang Hongli is stocking the vegetables. Impoverished due to illness, she is able to earn a salary of more than 1,000 yuan a month at the Philanthropic Supermarket.

07

08

07 “爱心超市”的员工彭亚乐（左）在帮顾客选购商品。

08 村民在余家花苑新村的“爱心超市”购物结账。

07 Peng Yale (left), an employee of the Philanthropic Supermarket, is helping a customer with shopping.

08 Paying at the register.

一位残疾企业家和他的残疾工友
A Disabled Entrepreneur and His Disabled Coworkers

图/文　郝群英
Photos and Text by Hao Qunying

因幼时患小儿麻痹症，王永刚落下了左下肢残疾的毛病。但他身残志坚，白手起家，创就了一番事业。

王永刚到建筑工地干过活，开过出租车，跟人合伙办过辣椒酱厂，还远赴云南送过冷饮，再到石家庄从事服装加工生意。借助家乡河北省邯郸市号召外出务工人员回乡创业的东风，在鸡泽县残联和乡党委、政府的支持和帮助下，王永刚凭借多年摸爬滚打的经验和掌握的流行服装技术，于2008年创建了东柳村第一家服装企业——鸿鹄服装有限公司。

他推行“公司+农户”生产经营模式，安置400多名残疾人到公司就业，带动周边乡村创建了服装、手套、箱包加工等摊点200多家，带动4000余名农村闲散劳动力就业创业，实现了带领群众共同致富的愿望。

感恩社会报桑梓，“八个免费”送乡亲。在他的企业，就餐免费、住宿免费、洗浴免费、技能培训免费、康复训练免费、阅览报刊免费、电动车和手机充电免费、上下班班车接送免费。看似简单的几个免费，合计下来，企业每年承担花销一二十万元。

王永刚把“诚信”贯穿于企业经营的全过程，如今公司成为年收入上千万的大型服装企业，他本人被评为河北省

Due to the after effect of poliomyelitis, Wang Yonggang became disabled in his left lower limb. However, with a strong will, he started his own business from scratch and became quite established.

Wang had been a construction worker and a taxi driver before trying his hand running his own business. He co-ran a chili sauce factory and delivered cold drinks before getting into a garment business in Shijiazhuang. Wang set up a fashion business in his home village in Handan City, Hebei Province in 2008, with the help of local authorities. Honghu Garments Co., Ltd. became the first fashion business in his home village of Dongliu.

Wang adopts a “company plus farmer” model in production and operation and employs over 400 workers with disabilities. Under his influence and guidance, over 200 small businesses including garments, gloves and suitcase manufacturing have been set up in surrounding villages and over 4,000 rural laborers either got employed or started their own businesses.

He is generous giving back to the community. All of his company employees are entitled to free meals, free accommodation, free bathing, free work skill training, free shuttle bus and free rehabilitation workout. These benefits alone cost his company about 200,000 yuan a year.

With the core operating philosophy of “good faith,” he has turned his company into a large garment enterprise earning an annual revenue of up to 10 million yuan. The company has won the title of “philanthropic enterprise” and has been named by the provincial government a “Provincial Exemplar Base for Employing Disabled People.” He himself has been recognized as Outstanding Entrepreneur of Jize County, Innovative Private En-

邯郸市鸡泽县全民创业先进个人、邯郸市发展民营经济创业功臣、河北省首批农村拔尖青年人才，公司成为省级残疾人就业扶贫示范基地，被省政府命名为“爱心企业”。

trepreneur of Handan City, and one of Hebei Province's Young Talents.

01

02

01 2014年5月14日，王永刚为一名下肢残疾的职工指导缝纫技术。

02 王永刚在公司车间里展示员工制作的产品。

01 Wang Yonggang teaching sewing skills to a disabled employee, May 4, 2014.

02 Products by his workshop.

03

04

05

03 鸡泽县鸿鹄服装有限公司设有无障碍通道为残疾职工提供方便。

04 2014年5月14日，在公司残疾职工培训班上，老师向残疾职工传授缝纫技能。

05 残疾职工在公司的康复室进行康复训练。

03 Accessible passage makes it easy for employees of Honghu Garments.

04 At a sewing skill training class on May 14, 2014.

05 Rehabilitation training room of the company.

06 2014年5月14日，王永刚（右一）和职工将邯郸市残联颁发的“邯郸市残疾人扶贫基地”牌匾挂到公司门前。

07 王永刚从公司围墙外的标语“莫道今日创业难，笑看来日富裕甜”前走过。

06

07

06 On May 14, 2014, Wang Yonggang (first right) and his employees putting up a plaque that says “Handan City Poverty Alleviation Base for the Disabled” conferred by the Handan City Federation of Disabled Persons.

07 Wang Yonggang walks past a slogan on the wall of his company that encourages people to work hard.

发挥东西部扶贫协作和中央单位定点帮扶的引领示范作用，凝聚国际国内社会各方面力量，进一步提升贫困人口帮扶精准度和帮扶效果，形成脱贫攻坚强大合力。

——《“十三五”脱贫攻坚规划》

We will give full play to the exemplary role of cooperation between eastern and western regions and the leading role of central government agencies in poverty alleviation. We need to integrate resources from all social sectors, domestic and foreign, and further promote targeted assistance for the impoverished so that a great momentum can be developed to overcome poverty.

——National Plan for Poverty Alleviation During the 13th Five-Year Plan Period (2016-2020)

八方支援　众志成城

社会扶贫

Alleviating Poverty by Mobilizing Social Resources

不易的前行——定点扶贫记

Targeted Poverty Alleviation in Designated Areas Through the State Banking System

图/文　杨凯生
Photos and Text by Yang Kaisheng

1995年起，按照国务院有关部门的统一安排，中国工商银行陆续与四川省通江县、南江县、达州的万源市、凉山州的金阳县建立定点帮扶关系。工商银行积极落实“精准扶贫、精准脱贫”部署，建立健全金融精准扶贫工作机制，创新金融扶贫模式，加大各类资源投入力度，瞄准靶向精准发力积极助推四川省的脱贫攻坚工作。

工商银行与当地党委、政府和人民群众一起，积极帮助当地改变贫困面貌，走出了一条金融扶贫、产业扶贫、教育扶贫、卫生扶贫相结合的扶贫开发新路子，帮助当地朝着生产发展、生活富裕、生态良好的可持续发展方向前进，助推当地社会进步和经济发展，惠及四川数百个乡村和十余万贫困群众。工商银行和辖属的四川分行先后被国务院扶贫办评为定点扶贫工作先进单位。

Since 1995, at the direction of the State Council, the Industrial and Commercial Bank of China (ICBC) has worked consecutively with Tongjiang County, Nanjiang County, Wanyuan City and Jinyang County to establish designated poverty alleviation service relationships. The ICBC has taken measures for targeted poverty alleviation, including improving relevant financial mechanisms, creating new financial models, and increasing investment of various resources.

The ICBC has worked closely with the local Party committee, government and people in the drive to change the status quo and has trailblazed a new path of poverty alleviation through the joint effort of the financial, industrial, educational and health care sectors – a path of sustainable development featuring high productivity, high standard of living, and sound eco-environment. The endeavor has promoted local social progress and economic development and has benefited over 100,000 poverty-stricken people in several hundred Sichuan villages. The ICBC and its Sichuan branch have been successively honored by the State Council Leading Group Office of Poverty Alleviation and Development as “Model Institution of Targeted Poverty Alleviation.”

01

02

01 通往巴中通江县陈河乡陈家坝村小学的路上有条河，以前河上没有桥，村里20多名学生上学、放学要靠父母接送。学校老师则承担起背送孩子们过河的重任。

02 李佐英老师在工商银行捐资修建的“爱心桥”上为学生整理衣装。

01 A river on the way to the Chenjiaba Village Elementary School in Chenhe Township, Tongjiang County, Bazhong. Since there was no bridge across the river, more than 20 students in the village had to be walked to and back from school by their parents and the teachers had to carry these children on their backs to get across the river.

02 Li Zuoying doing up one of her students' clothes as they cross the new bridge built with donated funds from ICBC.

03

04

05

03 通江县陈河乡中小学学生在体育场上跑步。该学校是工商银行最早在四川定点帮扶的学校。

04 陈河乡中小学学生在科学实验室上课。1997年开始，工商银行先后捐资对陈河乡中小学原教学综合楼进行加层，扩建教室和教师宿舍。近年又平整了运动场，新建了学生厨房，建成了多媒体教室，添置了课桌椅，购置了一批体育器材和图书。

05 位于巴中市通江县的巴山生态牧业科技有限公司总经理张育贤正在讲述产业扶贫新模式。工商银行生态养殖扶贫项目创新了“工行+政府扶贫部门+村党支部+龙头企业+建档立卡贫困户”+保险的“5+1”发展模式，由工商银行年捐资从龙头企业购买仔猪提供给贫困户；龙头企业负责技术指导、疫病防治，引入保险机制；扶贫部门负责立项监督，驻村第一书记负责日常管理；龙头企业负责兜底回购；工行融e购帮助企业拓展销售渠道。

03 Students of Chenhe Township School in Tongjiang County running along a playground track. It was the first school in Sichuan built with ICBC donations.

04 A science class at Chenhe Township School. Since 1997, ICBC has sponsored the school's renovation of a teaching building and a teachers' dorm, leveling the playground, building a students' canteen and multi-media classrooms, and buying new desks and chairs, sporting facilities and books.

05 Zhang Yuxian, general manager of Bashan Ecological Animal Husbandry Technology Co., Ltd., explains a new model of poverty alleviation through industrial development. The model involves cooperation among five parties: ICBC, the government's poverty-relief departments, village Party branches, leading enterprises, poverty-stricken households, and insurance companies. ICBC buys piglets from enterprises for the poverty-stricken households; the enterprises help with technical guidance, disease control and treatment, and arrange insurance coverage; the government departments take care of project approval and supervision; the chief secretary takes charge of routine management; the enterprises purchase all raised pigs; and the ICBC e-finance platform helps the enterprises expand distribution channels.

06

06 巴山生态牧业科技有限公司职工在为青峪猪添加饲料。该公司在种猪选育、小猪繁育、育肥猪养殖、生猪屠宰、产品精分割、产品精深加工、冷链物流运输、产品销售等全产业链中坚持绿色、有机、环保的理念。

06 Pigs being fed by an employee of Bashan Ecological Animal Husbandry Technology Co., Ltd.

07

07 工行扶贫干部帮助简文波喂牛。万源市茶垭乡老洼坪村简文波是外地嫁过来的媳妇，几年前，她依靠工商银行的16万元贷款开始养牛。

08 “简文波菜牛养殖场”现养牛40多头，还养了一批黑鸡。她希望工商银行给她的贷款期限稍微延长一点，“现在卖牛还贷款的话，赚得太少，划不来。”

08

07 An ICBC poverty alleviation worker helps Jian Wenbo feed the cattle. Jian settled down in Laowaping Village, Chaya Township, Wanyuan City after getting married here. Several years ago, she got into the cattle raising business with a loan of 160,000 yuan from ICBC.

08 Currently, Jian Wenbo raises over 40 heads of cattle and a herd of black chicken. She hopes she can have a grace period for loan payment from ICBC because she has a cash flow problem.

09

09 南江县下两镇瓦坪村贫困户彭新昌以前的家。

10 彭新昌吆喝羊群入圈。他现在有了新房子和一个增收产业园，养了羊、鸡，种了茶园和万寿菊。

09 Former residence of Peng Xinchang, an impoverished person in Waping Village, Xialiang Town, Nanjiang County.

10 Peng Xinchang summons his sheep into their fold. He now has a new house, raises sheep and chicken and plants tea and marigolds.

10

11

12

11 2016年，金阳县委常委、副县长、工商银行扶贫干部韩建设在丙底乡木尼古尔村建档立卡贫困户土比土哈家中走访调研。这是他第三次来到丙底乡，目的是为了推动捐资10万元与政府合作在木尼古尔村成立以养牛为主的集体经济项目。土比土哈家盼着养牛项目能为他们家带来些收入。

12 土比土哈展示挂晒在房子顶棚里的过年肉。如今，他家里也搞了种养殖，日子逐渐好过起来。

11 In 2016, Han Jianshe, Jinyang County deputy mayor, visiting for the third time Tubi Tuha and his family, a documented impoverished household in Munigu'er Village, Bingdi Township. Han is promoting a government-sponsored collective cattle-raising business in the village. He needs to raise 100,000 yuan for the project. Tubi Tuha and his family are hoping to benefit from the project.

12 Tubi Tuha shows cured pork hanging on the ceiling which is reserved for Chinese New Year. Animal husbandry has boosted his family income.

13

14

13 三年多前，南江县寨坡乡张荣才的父亲病重，他自身也缺乏劳动技术，生活十分贫困。工商银行让他参加了黄羊精准扶贫项目。

14 张荣才的生活变化不小，房屋已刷新。他觉得生活比过去有指望了。

13 Zhang Rongcai, a poor villager from Zhaipo Township, Nanjiang County, enrolled in a Mongolian gazelle raising project sponsored by ICBC.

14 Zhang Rongcai in front of his refurbished house.

核桃滞销直播来帮忙
Selling Walnuts on the Internet

图/文　高新生
Photos and Text by Gao Xinsheng

2017年12月23日，几名来自山西晋贡天下农特网、人人惠、本地头条、樱草频道等爱心企业的“晋贡天下扶农助农项目组”的工作人员，在山西运城市新绛县泽掌镇向家庄村，运用“直播+电商平台销售”的模式，帮助村民销售滞销的土特产干核桃。

几台手提电脑、一台打印机、一部手机、一名主播、一名摄像和几名工作人员，齐心协力，网络直播了一个多小时，邻村一对农民兄妹歌手现场献艺助阵，每单9斤98元的舌尖美食，吸引了全国各地爱心人士下订单。从22日发布直播消息至23日下午3时，爱心订单已达700多单，销售核桃6300多斤。

向家庄村曾以种植小麦、三樱椒和畜牧养殖为主，近年来转型发展经济核桃林1600多亩，产量达50万斤，成为当地增收的新产业。今年，受天气和市场影响，核桃首次出现滞销，村民愁眉不展。此次“互联网+直播+销售”的模式，帮了村民的大忙。

On December 23, 2017, sponsored by shanxi.gongtianxia.com, renrenhuiqq.com, benditoutiao.com, YingcaoFM and other enterprises, several members of the Shanxi Agricultural Product Sale Assistance Group came to Xiangjiazhuang Village, Zezhang Town, Xinjiang County, Shanxi Province. They helped the villagers sell dried walnuts, a local specialty, through “webcasting and e-business platform marketing.”

A brother and sister from a neighboring village gave singing performances to attract the audience as a webcaster, a cameraman and several assistants worked together with several laptops, a printer and a cellphone to market the walnuts. In less than two days, the group sold more than 3,150 kg of walnuts.

Villagers of Xiangjiazhuang used to make a living mainly by planting wheat and pod pepper and breeding livestock. In recent years, they transformed their development model and planted over 1,600 *mu* (around 107 hectares) of walnut trees with an annual yield of around 250,000 kg. The new venture has become a revenue booster for the local economy. This year, due to weather and market influence, walnuts became a hard sell for the first time. The online marketing campaign was certainly a big help to the worried villagers.

01

02

01 丰收的干核桃。
02 村民堆放土特产干核桃。

01 A harvest of dried walnuts.
02 The joy of harvest.

03

04

03 直播现场，村民向观众展示土特产干核桃。

04 工作人员用“直播+电商平台销售”的模式推销核桃。

05 邻村农民歌手在直播现场献歌助兴。

06 主播向观众“秀”爱心订单。

03 Villagers show their walnuts to the audience during webcasting.

04 Sales promotion of walnuts through webcasting and e-commerce.

05 A farmer from a neighboring village singing on webcast to appeal to the audience.

06 The webcaster shows off orders to the audience.

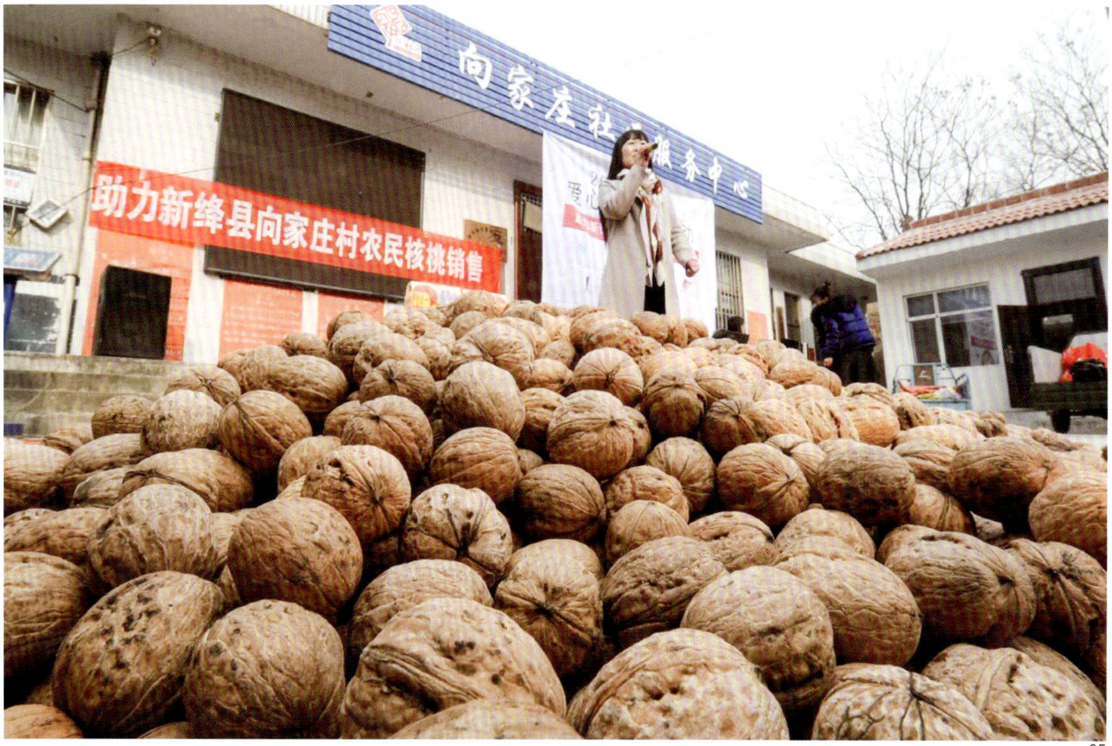
向家庄社 服务中心
助力新绛县向家庄村农民核桃销售
05

2017晋贡天下
爱心扶农助农活动
助力新绛县向家庄村农民核桃销售
06

爱心衣屋
Philanthropic Wardrobe

图/文 刘传福
Photos and Text by Liu Chuanfu

四川省泸州市“爱心衣屋”志愿者协会发起了“回收衣物、捐献他人”活动，将120个衣箱放置在该市纳溪区、泸县等地的小区和广场，大量回收居民闲置旧衣物，通过分类、清洗、包装等工序，做成“放心产品”，无偿捐献给全国各地的贫困群体，实现旧衣服多次循环使用，环保又利民。活动自2014年9月启动，在近两年时间里，吸纳了300余名志愿者加入，回收旧衣服10万余件，4.6万件衣服送达贵州、西藏、新疆等全国20余个县的3万多贫困群众家中。

The Philanthropic Wardrobe Volunteers' Association in Luzhou City, Sichuan Province launched a campaign to collect and recycle used clothes. They placed 120 clothes recycling trunks in communities and squares in Naxi District, Luxian County and other places to massively collect used clothes. Through sorting, cleaning, packaging and other procedures, these clothes are made into reusable products to be donated to impoverished people all over China. The reuse of clothes helps protect the environment and benefit the people. In about two years since the campaign was launched in September 2014, it involved over 300 volunteers, resulting in the recycling of over 100,000 used clothes, of which 46,000 have been sent to over 30,000 low-income people in over 20 counties in Guizhou, Tibet, Xinjiang and other parts of China.

01 2016年4月16日，泸州市纳溪区永宁街道较场坝社区的群众在“爱心衣屋”衣箱前捐献闲置衣物。
02 志愿者整理居民捐献的旧衣服。

01 People from the Jiaochangba Community, Naxi District, Luzhou City donating their used clothes, April 16, 2016.
02 Volunteers sorting out used clothes donated by residents.

01

02

03

03 志愿者将居民捐献的旧衣物进行消毒。

04 志愿者将居民捐献的旧衣物进行分类整理并贴上“爱心衣屋”标签。

03 Volunteers sterilizing used clothes donated by residents.

04 Volunteers sorting out used clothes donated by residents and put on the Philanthropic Wardrobe label.

04

05

06

05 志愿者将居民捐献的旧衣物分类别放置。
06 一名志愿者展示处理完毕的旧衣物。

05 Volunteers arranging the donated used clothes by category.
06 A volunteer showing packaged used clothes ready for shipping.

一名驻村干部的故事
The Story of an Official Temporarily Residing in a Village

图/文　杨文斌
Photos and Text by Yang Wenbin

台沙村位于贵州省黔东南苗族侗族自治州剑河县大山深处的南明镇，曾是当地典型的没有产业扶持的“空壳村”，村民们守着自家一亩三分地过日子。

2015年3月，53岁的共产党员杨精泽临危受命，被剑河县派往台沙村任“第一书记”。白天，杨精泽与村民们一起下地干活；晚上，他挑灯夜战，忙着写申请，做项目方案。杨精泽主动协调，在当地扶贫、水利、交通等相关部门的支持下，带领村民先后硬化了串寨路、篮球场，修建起鼓楼、垃圾站、娱乐场所，完善了基础设施。同时，组建起种养殖脱贫专业合作社，在荒山上种植钩藤、缬草等中药材，钩藤下实行土鸡、豪猪等特色养殖，稻田里套养“稻花鱼”，引导和带动贫困户加入合作社。

杨精泽驻村一年任期将满，20多名村民联名写申请书请求上级单位把杨精泽留下来。村民们的诚心打动了上级部门，也感动了杨精泽。杨精泽留了下来。

驻村这些年，杨精泽忙着为村里跑资金、争项目、完善基础设施，化解矛盾纠纷，为留守儿童申请助学金补助，村民都把他叫作“跑腿干部”。如今的台沙村，荒山变绿了，荒地重新种上了农作物。村民人均年收入由2014年杨精泽来驻村前的2200元，增加至2016年的3900元，“空壳村”变成产业村。

Taisha Village in Nanming Town located deep in the mountains of Jianhe County, Qiandongnan Miao and Dong Autonomous Prefecture, Guizhou Province, used to be a typical farming village with no industrial backup.

In March 2015, Yang Jingze, a 53-year-old CPC member, was appointed Party secretary of Taisha Village. By day, Yang worked in the fields with the villagers; by night, he did the paper work and drafted project proposals. With support from local authorities of poverty alleviation, water resources, transportation and other related departments, Yang led the villagers to improve the infrastructure by paving the roads and the basketball court, build a drum tower, a garbage station and a recreational center. Meanwhile, he organized a specialized planting and livestock raising cooperative for poverty alleviation to plant uncaria, valerian and other medicinal herbs on deserted hills, to breed chickens, porcupines and other special animals, and to raise fish in rice fields.

When Yang Jingze was about to finish his one-year-long tenure, over 20 villagers jointly wrote a letter to appeal to the higher authorities to renew his term of office. The sincerity of the villagers moved the authorities and Yang himself. So he stayed on serving as Party secretary.

During his stay in the village, Yang has earned himself the title of “errand official” because of the many things he has done for the villagers, including applying for funds, seeking projects, improving the infrastructure, resolving conflicts, applying for grants and subsidies for left-behind children. Today, Taisha Village has turned on a new leaf. Its deserted hills have turned green and its barren fields are full of crops. The villagers' annual income per capita increased from 2,200 yuan in 2014 to 3,900 yuan in 2016. The previously pure agrarian village has changed into an industrial village.

In July 2016, Yang Jingze was awarded the honorary title of

2016年7月，杨精泽被黔东南州委授予“全州优秀共产党员”称号；2017年5月，他又被贵州省总工会授予“贵州省五一劳动奖章”。“这是鼓励，也是责任，将鞭策我去做得更好。”杨精泽说。

"Model CPC Member" by the Qiandongnan Prefecture Party Committee, and in May 2017, he was awarded the "Guizhou Provincial May 1st Labor Medal" by the Guizhou Provincial Labor Union.

01

02

01 2017年6月7日，杨精泽与村民在台沙村种养殖脱贫专业合作社里喂鸡。
02 杨精泽在台沙村种养殖脱贫专业合作社的辣椒地里给村民传授辣椒管护技巧。

01 Yang Jingze (left) feeding the chickens with a villager at the cooperative specializing in planting and livestock raising for poverty alleviation in Taisha Village, June 7, 2017.
02 Yang Jingze teaching the villagers how to take care of hot pepper plants.

03

03 杨精泽（右一）与村民在合作社的辣椒地里松土、除草。
04 杨精泽（前）与村民劳动归来走在群山绿野间。

03 Yang Jingze (first right) and fellow villagers working in the hot pepper field.
04 Going home after a day's work.

04

05

06

05 结束一天的劳动，杨精泽（左二）与村民们一同回家。
06 在合作社的稻田里插秧时杨精泽不慎被蚂蟥叮咬。

05 On the way home.
06 Yang Jingze got bit by a leech while planting rice.

07

08

09

07 杨精泽（左一）到剑河县扶贫办递交扶贫项目申请材料。
08 杨精泽（蓝衣者）与村民开会讨论合作社土地流转问题。
09 杨精泽（左二）和村干部深入农户家中做产业发展情况回访调查。

07 Yang Jingze (first left) applying for approval for a poverty alleviation project at the Jianhe County Poverty Alleviation Office.
08 Yang Jingze (in blue) is having a meeting with villagers to discuss land transfer.
09 Yang Jingze (second left) doing research in a farmer's home.

10

10 杨精泽（蓝衣者）与村民共进午餐。
11 杨精泽一年的驻村服务期满后，村民们联名盖手印向上级部门申请，让他留下来。

10 Having lunch with villagers.
11 Villagers' written petition to renew Yang Jingze's term of office.

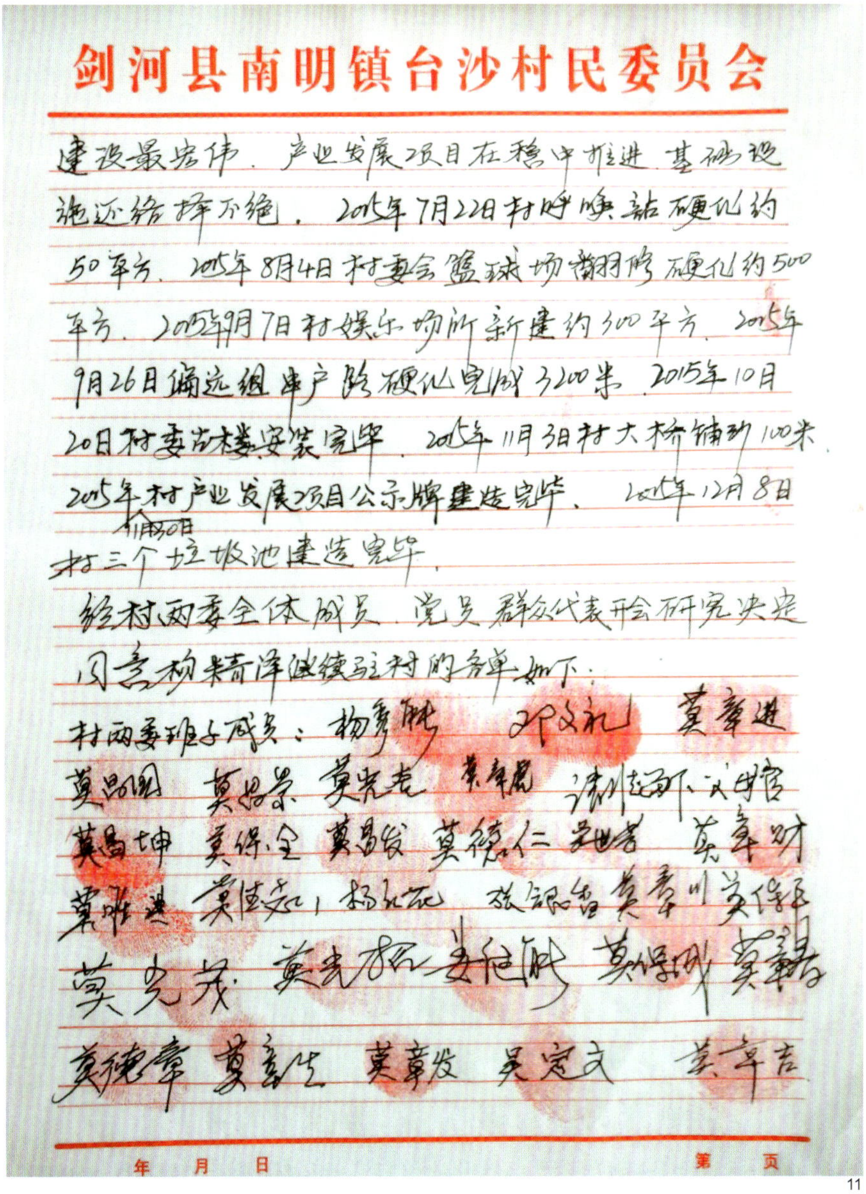

剑河县南明镇台沙村民委员会

建设最宏伟，产业发展项目在稳中推进，基础设施还络绎不绝。2015年7月22日村晒谷坪硬化约50平方，2015年8月4日村委会篮球场翻修硬化约500平方，2015年9月7日村娱乐场所新建约300平方，2015年9月26日偏远组串户路硬化完成3200米，2015年10月20日村委会办公楼安装完毕，2015年11月3日村大桥铺砂100米，2015年11月30日村产业发展项目公示牌建造完毕，2015年12月8日村三个垃圾池建造完毕。

经村两委全体成员、党员、群众代表开会研究决定同意杨精泽继续驻村的名单如下：

村两委班子成员：杨秀彬 邓文礼 莫章进 莫昌国 莫忠荣 莫光老 莫章胤 谢起邦 吴世信 莫昌坤 莫保全 莫昌发 莫德仁 吴世生 莫章财 莫兴进 莫佳元 杨秀荣 张银富 莫章州 莫保银 莫光荣 莫光标 姜维彬 莫保成 莫章培 莫德章 莫章先 莫章发 吴定文 莫章吉

年　月　日　　第　页

11

以革命老区、民族地区、边疆地区、集中连片特困地区为重点，整体规划，统筹推进，持续加大对集中连片特困地区的扶贫投入力度，切实加强交通、水利、能源等重大基础设施建设，加快解决贫困村通路、通水、通电、通网络等问题，贫困地区区域发展环境明显改善，“造血”能力显著提升，基本公共服务主要领域指标接近全国平均水平，为2020年解决区域性整体贫困问题提供有力支撑。

——《“十三五”脱贫攻坚规划》

With integrated planning, we will focus on alleviating poverty in the old revolutionary base areas, ethnic areas, border areas and contiguous areas of extreme poverty. In particular, we will devote intensified effort to alleviating poverty in the extremely impoverished contiguous areas. We will further build up major infrastructure facilities such as transportation, water conservancy and energy resources, accelerate solution of problems concerning access to roads, water, electricity and Internet connection in impoverished villages. We want to see noticeably improved conditions and regenerative capacity for regional development in poverty-stricken areas so that key indicators of basic public services may reach average national level, thus providing strong backup for overall poverty issues of a regional nature by 2020.

——National Plan for Poverty Alleviation During the 13th Five-Year Plan Period (2016-2020)

要输血　更要造血

提升贫困地区区域发展能力

Promoting Regenerative Capacity of Development in Poverty-stricken Areas

"绿色福利"惠及罗平石漠化地区

How Luoping County's Desert Area Has Benefited from Ecological Improvement

图/文 毛虹
Photos and Text by Mao Hong

云南省罗平县是典型的石漠化地区，石漠化面积2712.2平方公里，是全国14个连片特困地区，680个扶贫攻坚重点县之一。

2016年至2017年，罗平县投入43亿元用于精准扶贫工作，2018年初，罗平县退出贫困县序列。

在全县最贫困的村寨之一，地处冷凉山区的彝族村寨阿西者村，全村59户中建档立卡贫困户有32户。为彻底摆脱贫困，在当地政府的大力扶持下，2016年该村进行整体搬迁重建。目前，新村已基本建设完成。

在脱贫的同时，罗平县努力建设美丽宜居乡村，围绕"保护生态就是保护生命力，建设生态就是发展生产力"的发展理念，实施生态立县战略，大力推进退耕还林、天然林保护、防护林建设、石漠化治理等重点生态工程，让人民享受到更多"绿色福利"。

依靠当地优势资源，罗平县在产业扶贫方面取得成效。阿岗镇阿启村利用该村数万亩草场，引进龙头企业，采取"公司+基地+合作社+农户"模式，着力培育肉牛龙头企业，重点扶持养殖大户、合作社，以打造现代生态肉牛养殖业，将养牛与扶贫产业结合起来，解决全村扶贫产业滞后、项目规模小、成

Luoping County, Yunnan Province has a stony desertified area of 2,712.2 square kilometers. It is one of the 14 national contiguous areas of extreme poverty and one of China's 680 impoverished counties to be provided with focused assistance.

From 2016 to 2017, Luoping County devoted 4.3 billion yuan to targeted poverty alleviation. By the beginning of 2018, Luoping was no longer listed as a poverty-stricken county.

Axizhe, an ethnic Yi village situated in a cold region of high altitude, is one of the most impoverished villages in Louping. Thirty-two of its 59 households are documented impoverished. In order to eradicate poverty, the village was relocated and rebuilt in 2016 with strong support from the local government. Currently, the new village has basically been completed.

While working on poverty alleviation, Luoping County strives to make its villages environmentally friendly and liveable. Seeing eco-environmental protection as vitality protection and development of productivity, Luoping focused on providing people with "green benefits" by prioritizing ecological protection measures such as converting developed farmland back into forests, protecting natural forests, and building shelterbelts and stony desertification control.

Based on local resources, Luoping has made great strides in poverty alleviation by developing industry. Aqi Village in Agang Town used its huge acreage of pasture to attract investors and build up organic beef cattle companies and gave special support to major cattle breeders and cooperatives so as to increase productivity and income. Relying on the model of "business + base + cooperative + farmer," the county merged cattle breeding into

效不明显等问题，实现畜牧业增效和农民脱贫增收。

poverty alleviation industries and solved economic structural problem such as backwardness of industry, small project scale and lack of efficiency.

01

02

03

01 2016年年初，阿西者村原貌。
02 2017年9月，阿西者村新貌。
03 航拍阿西者村新貌。

01 Former look of Axizhe Village, early 2016.
02 New look of Axizhe Village, September 2017.
03 Aerial view of the new Axizhe Village.

04

05

06

07

04 2016年4月，脱贫摘帽后的小舟子村。
05 小舟子村成为“扶贫温饱示范村”。
06 小舟子村的新修小路和垃圾房。
07 小舟子村村民住进了漂亮的新房。

04 Xiaozhouzi Village after being lifted out of poverty, April 2016.
05 Xiaozhouzi Village has become a showcase of poverty alleviation.
06 A garbage chamber by a newly-built road in Xiaozhouzi Village.
07 Villagers of Xiaozhouzi Village have moved into beautiful new houses.

08

09

10

08 大片油菜花田使小舟子村充满绿色生机。
09 2017年8月31日，罗平县鲁布革乡绿意盎然。
10 2017年8月21日，阿启村草场上生态养殖的肉牛。

08 New houses by a large field of rape flowers.
09 Verdant green of Lubuge Township, Luoping County, Yunnan Province, August 31, 2017.
10 Grass-fed beef cattle on a green pasture in Aqi Village, August 21, 2017.

亦可妈库苗寨换新颜
A New Look of Yikemaku Ethnic Miao Village

图/文　适志宏
Photos and Text by Shi Zhihong

走进神奇的无量山间，沿着前往澜沧江边蜿蜒的山路崎岖前行，一座掩映在翠绿核桃林中享有典型苗族文化的崭新村落跃入眼帘。

云南省南涧彝族自治县碧溪乡亦可妈库苗族村共有28户112人，其中建档立卡贫困户6户26人。村民世代以打猎为生，散居在山里，生活条件比较艰苦。近年来，南涧县整合交通、民族团结示范村及农村危房改造等项目，实施安居保障、产业增收、基础设施等三大工程，推进全县苗族整族脱贫工作。据悉，该县投资850.74万元，对碧溪乡89户356人（其中建档立卡贫困户22户90人）实施苗族整族脱贫工作。随着脱贫攻坚政策不断落实，亦可妈库村村民全部按规划建起了漂亮的新居。

“过去，从杈杈房到毛草房变成土坯房，村中都是晴天一身灰，雨天一身泥。现在国家政策好，我们自己只花少部分钱，仅一年就把我们苗寨住了20多年的土坯房变成了漂亮的洋房，并修通水泥路，装上了路灯，家家户户用上自来水。政府还补助养牛、养猪、种果树，这样的好事以前做梦都没做着过。”70多岁的熊靖明说起山寨的变化十分激动。

Walking through a winding path in the fascinating Wuliang Mountain alongside the Lancang River, visitors will soon find a new village typical of ethnic Miao culture amid green walnut trees.

The Yikemaku Miao Village in Bixi Township, Nanjian Yi Autonomous County, Yunnan Province, has 112 people from 28 households. Of them, 26 are documented extremely impoverished people from six households. For generations, the villagers have lived a hard and isolated life in the mountain by hunting. In recent years, Nanjian County has integrated projects related to transportation, building of ethnic unity villages and renovation of dilapidated houses, and has launched programs aimed at guaranteed housing, increased industrial revenue and strengthened infrastructure so as to alleviate poverty of the entire ethnic Miao population in the whole county. The county has invested 8.5074 million yuan to help 356 people from 89 households in Bixi Township out of poverty, including 90 people from 22 households that are documented as extremely impoverished. As poverty alleviation policies were carried out step by step, all villagers of Yikemaku have built beautiful new houses as planned.

“In the past, we lived in thatched huts or mud brick houses and had to walk through dust on sunny days and mud on rainy days. Today, thanks to favorable state policy, we moved from more than two-decade-old mud brick houses into modern apartments within just one year, and we have concrete-paved roads, street lamps and potable tap water. The government even gives us subsidy raising cows and pigs and planting fruit trees. I didn’t even dream of all this!” said Xiong Jingming who is over 70.

01

02

01 苗寨寨门。
02 改造前的房屋外观。

01 Entrance to the Miao village.
02 Exterior of a house before renovation.

03

03 改造前简陋的厨房。
04 享有典型苗族文化的亦可妈库苗寨新景。

03 A pre-renovation kitchen.
04 A new and typical ethnic Miao village.

04

05

06

05 亦可妈库正在建设中的新房。
06 村民走在新修建的石板路上。

05 A new house in Yikemaku Village close to completion.
06 Villagers walking on a slab-paved road.

07

07 苗族群众家家户户用上自来水。
08 苗族群众在村寨的广场吹芦笙欢歌。

07 Each Miao household of the village has access to clean water.
08 Miao people singing and dancing on a village square.

08

09

10

09 苗族群众在活动广场跳舞。
10 苗族群众在户外做手工活儿。

09 Miao women dancing.
10 A Miao woman knitting.

11

11 村民赶着自家的牲口走在村中的石板路上。

11 Villagers driving their cattle through a slab-paved road.

12 政府兜底户杨正明夫妇的原住房。
13 杨正明夫妇的新住房。

12 Former residence of Yang Zhenming and his wife, who live on a government subsidy.
13 New house of the Yangs.

12

13

"悬崖村"藤梯变钢梯
Vine Ladder in "Cliff Village" Changed into Steel Ladder

图/文　饶国君
Photos and Text by Rao Guojun

通过改造房屋、建设电力、通讯设施，四川大凉山"悬崖村"正在改变。"悬崖村"精准扶贫路径也逐渐明朗——通过发展旅游文化产业，带动村民脱贫致富。6.3亿元将投入"悬崖村"用于修建空中索道、悬空栈道、悬崖天路、天村酒店等设施，将村子打造成特色彝家旅游新村。

"悬崖村"位于美姑河两岸，是典型的冲刷大峡谷地貌，生活在这里的彝族同胞共有680多人。需要攀爬悬崖的有阿土列尔村的阿土列尔、阿土特图2个村民小组，共计140多户、300多人。他们居住在平均海拔1400～1600米的断坎岩肩斜台上，出走山外全靠攀爬一条垂直落差800多米、蜿蜒长度为4公里的"藤条和木棒捆绑"的附岩悬梯，这些古朴的梯道共分17级、218步。据支尔莫乡党委书记阿皮几体介绍，阿土列尔村攀爬藤梯的历史可追溯到200多年前。

"悬崖村"第一书记帕查有格介绍说，州、县两级财政先后投入资金150多万元，将原来的藤梯换成钢梯。现在一条从山谷到山顶，总长度2.8公里，耗材120吨，累计设梯2556级，支搭钢管6000多节的"钢梯走廊"已全面建成。与原来的藤梯相比，钢梯裁弯取直、平稳好走，还有安全扶手，喷上防锈漆后寿命可达10至20年。由此，藤梯退出历史舞台。

要致富，先修路。通达问题是"悬

Through housing renovation, electric power and communication facilities building, "Cliff Village" in Daliang Mountain of Sichuan Province is putting on a new look. The village's targeted poverty alleviation is to develop tourism and cultural businesses. An investment of 630 million yuan will be used to build a cableway, a plank road, a cliff path and a hotel on the cliff. The aim is to develop it into a new tourism village with Yi ethnic characteristics.

"Cliff Village," located on the bank of the Meigu River, in a river-carved gorge, has an ethnic Yi population of over 680. Over 300 people from over 140 households live on the beveled shoulder of the cliff with an average altitude of 1,400 to 1,600 meters. To get connected to the outside world, they have to cross over the cliff through a ladder made of vines and wood sticks with a perpendicular height of over 800 meters and a total length of four kilometers. The vine ladder, which goes in 17 sections and 218 steps, had been used for 200 years, says Api Jiti, Party secretary of Zhi'ermo Township.

According to Pacha Yougé, chief Party secretary of "Cliff Village," the prefecture and county goverments invested over 1.5 million yuan to change the former vine ladder into the current steel ladder. Now, a "steel corridor" has been completed, spanning a total length of 2.8 kilometers from valley to peak and weighing a total of 120 tons, and composed of 2,556 steps and over 6,000 steel poles. Compared with the vine ladder, the steel ladder with painted safety railings is straight and can last up to 20 years. The days of using vine ladders are gone.

However, transportation is a still key livelihood issue for "Cliff Village." As cableways, highways and plank roads are being built, tourism projects of agritainment, rock climbing and valley adventure are also being implemented step by step. Villagers have begun planting walnut and chestnut trees, Chinese peppers and

崖村”目前还在继续的重点民生工程，随着建索道、修公路、布栈道等各项工作的开展，围绕旅游业开设避暑农家乐、健身攀岩行、探险峡谷游等项目也陆续推进。村民开始种植核桃、板栗、花椒、绿色蔬菜，提供给游客食用和购买，换取收入。“悬崖村”人均收入比5年前翻了一番，村民的精神文化生活极大改善，“悬崖村”以崭新的姿态喜迎八方游客！

green vegetables to sell to tourists and on the general market. Compared with the previous five years, villagers' per capita income has doubled, and their cultural life has been greatly enriched. Today, "Cliff Village" is welcoming visitors with a pleasing fresh look!

01

02

01 “悬崖村”原来悬崖峭壁上的“附岩藤梯”。钢梯建成后，这条充满艰辛曲折的出山之路已被废弃。现仅剩陡峭山壁上的3段，约50米。

02 “悬崖村”的孩子经过钢梯下山去学校。

01 A disused "cliff ladder." After the steel ladder was built, this arduous winding path to the outside world is no longer in use. Only three sections of the vine ladder with a length of about 50 meters are left today.

02 Children going downhill to school via the steel ladder.

03

03 “悬崖村”的孩子们结伴攀行钢梯去学校。

03 Going down the steel ladder to school.

04

04 “悬崖村”的孩子从学校回家时走在悬崖绝壁的钢梯上，翻过山头便是家。

04 Home is on the other side of the mountain.

05 从“悬崖村”远眺峡谷谷底扩建的学校。学校是寄宿制的，偎依在美姑河边。

05 A view of the cliff and the expanded boarding school in the valley by the Meigu River.

05

06 “悬崖村”架设的进山索道开通试运行，这条几乎与山体垂直的悬空索道投资上千万元，目前可运送300公斤以内的货物并提升到1000米峡谷。出于安全不载人上下。

07 “悬崖村”彝族同胞家家户户用上光伏发电，通过地面卫星接收器收看电视节目。通过建设电力设施，“悬崖村”有了很大变化。

06 Trial run of a cableway installed. Almost perpendicular to the mountain range, the 10-million-yuan cableway can currently lift 300 kilograms of goods to 1,000 meters up the valley. For the sake of safety, it is not used to carry people.

07 Each Yi household now has access to photovoltaic power and to TV programs via ground satellite receivers. The village saw big change after the building of photovoltic power facilities.

06

07

08

09

10

08 “悬崖村”村民在火堆边与游客聊天。攀越钢梯进村的游客、志愿者和支教人员，来开展社会调查，进行帮教支教，了解彝民文化，推动“悬崖村”发展。村里的农家乐接待游客，增加了收入，村民迅速脱贫，更关键的是由此带来了文化、观念的融合碰撞。

09 “悬崖村”的彝族同胞在做农家饭招待游客。随着大量游客的到来，勤劳的彝家妇女开始提升餐饮水平，特色的农家菜也要征求客人的口味。

10 “悬崖村”的一名妇女在喂养黑山猪。这里家家户户都有黑山猪，主要用青菜头、草食饲养。村民宰杀拿来招待游客，一只乳猪200—300元，增加了村民的家庭收入。

08 Villagers chatting with tourists by bonfire. The influx of tourists and volunteers through the steel ladder has promoted the village's economic development and cultural exchange with the outside world.

09 Ethnic Yi people cooking a homemade meal for tourists.

10 A woman feeding black pigs with vegetable scraps and fodder. Pigs are butchered to serve tourists and earn income. A porket can sell up to 300 yuan.

11

11 “悬崖村”村民某色拉洛的女儿某色杨花在家门前的树上“荡秋千”。

11 Family fun on a “swing.”

新疆最高公路大桥——果子沟大桥
Guozigou Bridge, the Highest Highway Bridge in Xinjiang

图/文　留光驻影（图01-02）、路海龙（图03）、汪铁锁（图04）、周常乐（图05）、孙自法（图06）、汤桂珍（图07）、陈晓锋（图08）
Photos and text by Liuguang Zhuying (Photos 01-02), Lu Hailong (Photo 03), Wang Tiesuo (Photo 04), Zhou Changle (Photo 05), Sun Zifa (Photo 06), Tang Guizhen (Photo 07) and Chen Xiaofeng (Photo 08)

果子沟大桥是中国连霍高速公路赛里木湖至果子沟高速公路（赛果高速公路）标志性工程，是新疆第一高桥，也是中国国内首座双塔双索钢桁梁公路斜拉桥。

大桥集新技术、新结构、新工艺、新设备于一体，是新疆公路建设史上一次重大突破。大桥全长700米，大桥跨径330米，主塔高度分别为209米和215.5米，在设计施工中，秉承"以最小限度破坏、最大限度的恢复"的环保理念，在克服地质灾害频发影响通行的同时，边施工边进行环保恢复工作。建成的大桥桥身与果子沟的美景浑然一体，为果子沟国家级风景区再添一道美丽风景线。

伊犁河谷地区煤炭资源丰富，是新疆四大煤炭资源基地之一。果子沟特大桥的建设和赛果高速公路的通车，提升了中亚大通道的便捷性，提升了伊犁地区经济前突位置功能，降低了伊犁地区农副产品外运时的损耗率，有效提高经济效益，也解决了伊犁河谷的出行难问题，使伊犁州能够全天候通达乌鲁木齐，对边疆地区的稳定和经济发展具有重大意义。

Guozigou Bridge is a landmark project on the Sayram-Guozigou Expressway, part of the Lianyungang-Khorgas Expressway. It is the highest bridge in Xinjiang and the first cable-stayed highway bridge of steel girder with parallel towers and cables.

Featuring a combination of new technology, new structure, new craftsmanship and new equipment, the bridge marks a breakthrough in the history of highway construction in Xinjiang. With a span of 330 meters and a length of 700 meters, and its main towers standing 209 and 215.5 meters tall, respectively, the bridge has become a new landmark of the Guozigou National Scenic Area. In both design and construction, the eco-environmental protection principle of "minimum damage and maximum restoration" was followed. Faced with frequent geological hazards, builders built the bridge in step with ecological restoration.

The Ili Valley area has large coal reserves and serves as one of the four major bases of coal in Xinjiang. Both the Guozigou Bridge and commissioning of the Sayram-Guozigou Expressway have greatly improved the functionality of the Central Asia transport corridor, lifted up the economic role of the Ili area, lowered the waste rate of agricultural and sideline products in the shipping link and effectively boosted economic returns. In addition, the bridge has solved the problem of travel bottlenecks in the Ili Valley area and have made it possible for travelers in Ili Prefecture to reach Urumqi at any time of the day, which is significant to the stability and economic development in this frontier area.

01

02

01 2008年5月27日，施工中的果子沟大桥Z1主塔。
02 2008年5月27日，果子沟大桥施工工地上，工人在Z1主塔上作业。

01 Z1 Main Tower of Guozigou Bridge under construction, May 27, 2008.
02 A worker working on the Z1 Main Tower, May 27, 2008.

03

03 2010年8月，果子沟大桥经过四年紧张施工，工程进入最后建设阶段，即将完成主桥合龙。
04 2011年，在建的果子沟大桥。

03 Guozigou Bridge in its final phase, August 2010.
04 Guozigou Bridge in 2011, during its 5th year of construction.

04

05 2011年12月11日，果子沟大桥冬日景观。

06 2013年8月12日，果子沟大桥跨越崇山峻岭。

05 Winter view of Guozigou Bridge, December 11, 2011.

06 Guozigou Bridge over mountain ridges, August 12, 2013.

05

06

07

08

07 2016年5月30日晚，果子沟大桥和公路交相辉映。
08 2017年4月21日，果子沟大桥雄姿。

07 Evening view of bridge and highway, May 30, 2016.
08 Guozigou Bridge, April 21, 2017.

中国的精准扶贫政策，以每年减贫1300万人以上的成就，书写了人类反贫困斗争史上“最伟大的故事”，赢得了国际社会的高度赞誉。中国新闻社图片网络中心作为中国两大通讯社之一中国新闻社的下属部门，以图片的形式，持续关注着精准扶贫的进展。

因此，当本书策划构思并最终确定下来之时，中国新闻社记者以及图片网络中心网站平台“中国新闻图片网”（www.cnsphoto.com）的签约摄影师在日常供稿中提供的大量关于中国扶贫的图片，成为本书内容筛选的基础。同时，为了丰富图片故事，我们在前期开展了“难忘脱贫攻坚”摄影作品及脱贫故事征集及评选活动，以期能从更广的范围、更基层的角度、更贴近扶贫前沿的视角，反映中国扶贫的情况和成果。

从初期征集到终稿，我们经历了征集、筛选、替换、再编辑的过程。囿于篇幅，我们不得不一次次忍痛割爱，舍弃了不少精彩故事，免不了有遗珠之憾；同时也深深地感到，本书所录之内容，覆盖面远远不及中国扶贫所及之范围。只能在权衡故事代表性、图片精彩度的基础上，从章节内容交叉重叠性、地域和民族分布等维度，尽可能地平衡取舍。一些来自于大众的图片故事在艺术性上跟专业摄影师还有一定差距，但在反映扶贫的层面上具有一定的代表性，权衡之下，本书亦予以收录。

本书凝聚了众多拍摄者的辛勤付出和努力，在此，特别感谢中国新闻社记者的图片作品支持，感谢大众积极投稿参与前期的征稿活动，感谢你们贡献了众多精彩的图片故事；感谢中国新闻高级记者王永志先生给本书内容提出了宝贵的建议，感谢图片网络中心各位同事的支持和付出，尤其是画刊部编辑朱兵先生在征稿过程中付出了大量的时间和精力；感谢中国外文局新世界出版社的大力支持和帮助，尤其是外宣编辑部主任李晨曦女士和责任编辑李莎莎女士的建议和敦促，你们的付出最终让本书得以顺利出版。

卷末回望，想起本书编写过程中的点滴，有遗憾，有不足，更有欣慰。凡是过去，皆为序曲。本书终于杀青，而中国的扶贫还在进行，任重而道远。记录亦将继续。我们将一如既往，继续追踪扶贫攻坚中的精彩故事，以影像聚焦扶贫，反映社会发展，记录历史温度，持续传递正能量，让共同担负的社会责任轮廓更加清晰，让齐心推动社会前进的步伐更趋一致。

编者

2018年6月

Postscript

Since initiating its targeted poverty alleviation policy, China has written its greater stories in the history of human struggle against poverty and has won acclaim from the international community for its annual record of relieving over 13 million people of poverty. The Photo Network Center of China News Service (CNS, one of the largest news agencies in China) has taken photographs to show progress and development of targeted poverty alleviation.

Therefore, by the time the planning of this book was finalized, the large number of photos about poverty alleviation in China provided regularly by CNS reporters and contract photographers of www.cnsphoto.com, the official website of the Photo Network Center, became the basic source of this book. Meanwhile, we carried out a nationwide contest for the best photos and stories that reflect China's status quo and achievements in poverty relief in a wider scope and from a grassroots perspective.

From the first photo down to the last draft, we have been through a long process of collecting, selecting, substituting and re-editing. Given the limited size of the book, we had to painfully give up many good stories during the editing process. If we could, we would certainly have presented a more wide-ranging view of the poverty alleviation effort. However, we did do our best striking a balance in the dimensions of context, coherence, and geographical and ethnic distribution after taking representativeness and attractiveness of the stories and photos into account. Some of the photographs included may not look as professional as they should be, but they are rather representative in terms of reflecting poverty alleviation in different strata of society.

This book is the result of many people's joint effort. We are especially obliged to CNS reporters for their pictures, and no less grateful to the public for their active contribution and participation in the preliminary photo contest. We want to thank Mr. Wang Yongzhi, former director of the CNS Department of Economic Affairs, for his valuable advice. We want to thank our colleagues at the CNS Photo Network Center for their photo contribution and other support. Our thanks also go to Mr. Zhu Bing of the CNS Pictorial Editing Department for his precious time and effort spent during the photo contest. We are also thankful to New World Press (NWP) for their great support, and especially to Ms. Li Chenxi (director) and Ms. Li Shasha (editor-in-charge) of the NWP's Editorial Office of International Communication, for their kind suggestions and due diligence. Thank all of you for making this book happen!

Closing this book here, we have mixed feeling of delight and regret (for possible blemishes), but all that is done is just the prelude to a new beginning. This book is finally done, but poverty alleviation in China is still ongoing and has a long way to go. So the job of record keeping will continue. We will keep tracking the great stories of the poverty reduction drive with video and visual images, reproduce the process of social development, work together to bring the contours of social responsibility to greater light and make sure no one is left behind as we make concerted effort to bring social development to higher levels.

CNS Photo Network Center

June 2018

图书在版编目（CIP）数据

图说中国梦. Ⅳ, 扶贫的故事 ： 汉英对照 / 中国新闻社图片网络中心主编 ； 么文浩译. -- 北京 ： 新世界出版社, 2018.8
ISBN 978-7-5104-6589-5

Ⅰ. ①图… Ⅱ. ①中… ②么… Ⅲ. ①中国历史－近现代－摄影集 Ⅳ. ①K25-64

中国版本图书馆CIP数据核字(2018)第199073号

图说中国梦Ⅳ：扶贫的故事

作　　者：中国新闻社图片网络中心
特邀主编：王　旻
总 策 划：李新洲　李晨曦
执行主编：石艺媛
翻　　译：么文浩
英文定稿：王池英　韩清月
责任编辑：李莎莎　李晨曦
封面设计：魏芳芳
版式设计：魏　丹
责任印制：王宝根　苏爱玲
出版发行：新世界出版社
社　　址：北京市西城区百万庄大街24号(100037)
发 行 部：(010)6899 5968　(010)6899 8705（传真）
总 编 室：(010)6899 5424　(010)6832 6679（传真）
网　　址：http://www.nwp.cn
http://www.nwp.com.cn
版 权 部：+8610 6899 6306
版权电邮：nwpcd@sina.com
印　　刷：北京东方宝隆印刷有限公司
经　　销：新华书店
开　　本：889mm×1194mm　1/16
字　　数：270千字　印张：15
版　　次：2018年8月第1版　2018年8月第1次印刷
书　　号：ISBN 978-7-5104-6589-5
定　　价：168.00元